What works in strategic partnerships for children?

Other titles in the series

What works in strategic partnerships for children?

Janie Percy-Smith

Published by Barnardo's
Tanners Lane
Barkingside
Ilford
Essex
IG6 1QG

Charity registration no 216250

First published 2005

Designed and produced by Andrew Haig & Associates

Printed in the United Kingdom by Russell Press, Nottingham

A catalogue record for this book is available from the British Library

ISBN 1 904659 10 1

Contents

List of boxes and figures

About the author

Janie Percy-Smith is an independent researcher and Visiting Professor at Leeds Metropolitan University where she was, until 2002, Professor of Public Policy. Janie has more than 15 years' experience of research and consultancy in the areas of research impact, social exclusion, local governance, regeneration and community development. She has particular expertise in relation to project and programme evaluation and qualitative research methods, and has worked extensively on projects requiring a high level of community involvement.

Recent publications include: *Improving the use of research in social care practice* (2004, with I Walter, S Nutley, D McNeish, S Frost), *Promoting change through research: the impact of research on local government* (2002), *Local governance in Britain* (2001, with R Leach), *Policy responses to social exclusion. Towards inclusion?* (2000).

Acknowledgements

I would like to thank Angela Hutton for her support during the writing of this research review. In the early stages of the research review Barnardo's organised a seminar for academics and practitioners in which I was able to 'test out' some preliminary findings. The discussion at this seminar was extremely helpful and I would like to thank all those who participated in that event. Finally, thanks to those people who kindly read the draft review and gave me helpful comments.

1 Introduction and policy context

Partnership working is now the preferred means of delivering a range of policies, programmes and projects. It has become especially important in relation to tackling complex problems that are perceived to be intractable and not amenable to resolution by any one agency working alone. Partnership working is not a new development but one that has gathered pace over the last two decades. It has not emerged as a 'good idea' within a political or policy vacuum. Rather it has been developed as a response to particular policy problems and contexts.

Exhortations to partnership working, integration, co-ordination and collaboration are commonplace across a wide range of quite different policy areas and, of particular interest to this publication, in relation to policies aimed at children and young people:

> Promoting children's well-being and safeguarding them from significant harm, depends crucially upon effective information sharing, collaboration and understanding between agencies and professionals. At the strategic level, agencies and professionals need to work in partnership with each other and with service users, to plan comprehensive and co-ordinated children's services. (Department of Health et al, 1999, p12)

The focus on partnership working is not surprising given the long list of high-profile failures to adequately 'join up' policy and practice epitomised most recently by the inquiry into the death of Victoria Climbié. However, commonplace, too, are the much less high profile day-to-day frustrations of children, young people and their families as they grapple with multiple providers in their efforts to secure appropriate and accessible services to meet their often complex and multi-faceted needs (see for example, Audit Commission, 2003a).

In this introductory chapter we examine the current policy context in relation to partnership working and children and young people. We then go on to look at the recent history of partnership working more generally, with a focus on those aspects of the policy and political context that have provided the impetus for partnership working. Finally, the scope of the remainder of the book is sketched out.

Children and young people – the policy context

Since 1997, it can be argued, children and young people have moved higher and higher up the political and policy agenda. There have been a plethora of initiatives aimed at addressing various aspects of children and young people's lives. At the same time there is continuing evidence of the extent of poverty and disadvantage experienced by many hundreds of thousands of children in Britain (see, for example, Bradshaw, 2001 and 2002; Howarth et al, 1999; Rahman et al, 2000 and 2001; Sutherland et al, 2003). The political salience and importance in policy terms of children and young people is reflected in the Green Paper, *Every child matters*, published in September 2003 (HM Treasury, 2003) which incorporates the government's response to the Laming Inquiry's report into the death of Victoria Climbié, and the subsequent Children Act 2004. The main theme of the recommendations of the Laming Inquiry report (Department of Health/Home Office, 2003) was the need to change fundamentally the way in which services for children are organised and delivered so that the failures of inter-agency communication which were identified by the Laming Inquiry would not be repeated.

However, this was by no means the first time that failures of agencies to collaborate had resulted in the death, injury or abuse of a child. Leiba and Weinstein cite two pieces of research reviewing child abuse inquiry reports. In the first the researchers found that lack of clarity about professional roles played a part in the breakdown of collaboration between agencies in eight cases. In the second, a review of 40 reports of serious incidents of child abuse showed that lack of inter-agency working and inadequate sharing of information were two of the six most common shortcomings in professional practice. Indeed, of the 40 cases examined, in only three could fault be laid at the door of a single individual or agency (Leiba and Weinstein, 2003, p75).

The Children Act 2004 sets out five outcomes for children and young people. The aim is to help all children and young people to:

- be healthy – enjoying good physical and mental health and living a healthy lifestyle
- stay safe – being protected from harm and neglect and growing up able to look after themselves
- enjoy and achieve – getting the most out of life and developing broad skills for adulthood

- make a positive contribution – to the community and to society and not engaging in anti-social or offending behaviour
- achieve economic well-being (DfES, 2004, p25).

These aims will be achieved through a wide-ranging programme of change that will include the reorganisation of local children's services around the needs of children, young people and their families rather than professional boundaries. A key aspect of the changes is a strengthening of the requirement for agencies across sectors to work together to improve the (shared) outcomes for children and young people.

The rationale for the changes proposed is what is described as the current frag-mentation of services for children at both local and national levels that can result in information not being shared across organisations and children slipping through the net; duplicated assessments; lack of co-ordination of the activities of the various agencies involved with a child; 'buck passing' between agencies; and lack of integra-tion of services:

> Our existing system for supporting children and young people who are beginning to expe-rience difficulties is often poorly coordinated and accountability is unclear. This means that information is not shared between agencies so that warning signs are not recognised and acted upon. Some children are assessed many times by different agencies and despite this may get no services. Children may experience a range of professionals involved in their lives but little continuity and consistency of support. Organisations may disagree over who should pay for meeting a child's needs because their problems cut across organisational boundaries. Fragmentation locally is often driven by conflicting messages and competing priorities from central Government. (HM Treasury, 2003, pp21–22)

The government proposes to address these issues through a series of structural and organisational changes designed to achieve both better integration of services and integration of organisations (see Miller, 2003 for a discussion of the organisational implications of the proposed changes). The Children Act 2004 requires local author-ities to enter into partnership arrangements with other key partners with reciprocal duties on them to co-operate. These partnership arrangements should:

- identify the needs, circumstances and aspirations of children and young people
- agree outcome goals and priorities for children and young people locally
- agree the contribution each agency should make to meeting these goals,

including through the effective sharing of information at a strategic level and about individual children and young people
- oversee arrangements for agencies to work together in the commissioning, delivery and integration of services, as appropriate (DfES, 2004, p15).

In the longer term the government is encouraging the integration of key services within Children's Trusts through the pooling of budgets and resources across local education authorities, children's social services, Connexions, certain health services and, where agreed locally, youth teams.

One area that will fall outside the boundaries of the Children's Trust is child protection. Currently this is managed strategically through non-statutory area child protection committees (ACPCs) which are multi-agency forums for agreeing and promulgating how the different services and professional groups should co-operate to safeguard children in the area and for making sure that arrangements work effectively to bring about good outcomes for children. However, a Joint Chief Inspectors' report (DfES et al, 2003) noted that these committees are not working well in some areas. As a result, the government has proposed that local authorities should have a duty to set up Local 'Safeguarding Children' Boards consisting of representatives from NHS bodies, the police, local probation boards, Connexions, local prisons, young offender institutions, the children and family court advisory and support services and lower tier councils with representation, as appropriate, from voluntary and community agencies. The Local Safeguarding Children Board will have the responsibility for co-ordinating and ensuring the effectiveness of local arrangements and services to safeguard children (DfES, 2004, pp15–16). This will build on the requirement, announced in September 2002, that local authority chief executives should take the lead in ensuring that all those responsible for planning, commissioning and delivering services for children and young people aged 0–19 should have agreed a local preventative strategy from April 2003, including systems for identification, referral and tracking (IRT) of children and young people at risk.

While fragmentation of planning and delivery of services has consequences at the local level, that fragmentation may originate at the national level as a result of, for example, separate targets emanating from different government departments, separate planning requirements, funding streams and inspection systems. Prior to the publication of the Green Paper the process of effecting better integration had begun with the appointment of a new Minister for Children, Young People and Families within the Department for Education and Skills. The minister has responsibility for a wide range of mainstream children's and young people's services, and special programmes and initiatives. This change was intended as the first step in a process of integrated policy development which will eventually involve a mechanism for setting outcomes and practice standards, building on standards for health and social care set out in the *National Service Framework for children, young people and maternity services* (Department of Health/Department for Education and Skills, 2004).

A key aspect of the standard-setting mechanism will be the rationalisation of targets to ensure that they are complementary across services and are focused on core outcomes (HM Treasury, 2003, p75). A further measure intended to improve integration and co-ordination is the creation of an integrated inspection framework across children's services. The new joint inspection framework will include assessment of how effectively services work together.

The related themes of partnership working, multi-disciplinary teams and integrated services to improve outcomes for children can be found throughout the Children Act 2004. As such the Act is arguably completing and formalising a process that began with the *Cross-cutting review of children at risk* (HM Treasury, 2001) which considered how best to ensure that support for children and young people and their families is better focused on preventative services. The goal was better co-ordination of services at local level so that when children are identified as facing risks there should be effective support early enough to address the problems before statutory intervention or acute services are necessary. The review made recommendations in three areas: delivering sustainable services; improving the inter-relationship between services; filling gaps and improving services for children at risk. These were then taken up as part of the 2002 Comprehensive Spending Review which recommended a three-pronged attack involving:

* strengthening existing local partnerships and piloting new children's trust models for integrated services
* better focusing of mainstream children and young people's services to ensure they respond better to those most in need
* early identification of need to ensure preventative services are available before children, young people and families hit crisis.

The Children and Young People's Unit (CYPU), set up in 2001, was given a particular remit to develop an overarching strategy covering all services for children and young people. Its strategy set out a number of principles and a vision of what services in the future will take account of and provide. The vision described in the CYPU's strategy document (Children and Young People's Unit, 2001a) makes specific reference to the need for excellent joined-up public services which strive to meet the needs of children, young people and their families. (The CYPU has been wound up following the restructuring of the new Children's and Families Directorate within DfES.) In its 2003 annual report the CYPU states:

> The Unit supports cross-Government work on child poverty and youth disadvantage, and covers the full 0–19 age range … CYPU doesn't lead on all child policy … instead we focus on cross-cutting issues that relate to more than just one aspect of a child's life and straddle more than just one Government department. (Children and Young People's Unit, 2003 p5)

One strand in delivering this vision was the setting up of a Children's Task Force in October 2000 to support policy-making and implementation of the NHS plan. It encompasses health, social care and public health policy for children and has been involved in the development of the National Service Framework (NSF) for children, young people and maternity services. It will demonstrate how agencies can work together to deliver services and ensure that care is child-centred, that appropriate services can be accessed at the right time and that children and families can take an active part in making decisions about their care.

The last 15 years has seen a plethora of new initiatives, many of them involving integration of key services and/or partnership working, aimed at children and young people (see Box A). However, the recent history of partnership working in relation to social care can, perhaps, be traced back to the Seebohm Committee report of 1969 which identified lack of co-ordination and integration within personal social services as a particular problem and proposed integration within a single executive agency – local authority social services departments. During the 1980s there was a counter-reaction to what were, by then, seen as large, inefficient bureaucracies and the introduction of new requirements to separate out purchaser and provider roles (see next section). The Children Act 1989 laid the foundations for joint working in relation to children and young people by including a section giving social services powers to call on the co-operation of education, health and housing authorities. The Health Act 1999 permitted the pooling of funds and in 2002 the Department of Health published guidance on producing children's plans which reinforced the idea of collaborative working by sanctioning the production of a single plan covering all aspects of children's services (Department of Health 2002c) (see also Gardner, 2003, p145 and Roaf, 2002, ch 1).

BOX A

Recent government policies requiring partnership working

England and Wales

1989: Children Act established statutory requirement for inter-agency collaboration in order to co-ordinate the planning of local services for children.

1998: Health White Paper, *Our healthier nation*, established requirements for improved partnerships between the NHS and local authorities.

1998: White Paper, *Modernising social services*, recommended improving partnerships to ensure more effective co-ordination of services for children through joint working between health, social services, housing and other services.

1998: Crime and Disorder Act established multi-agency youth offending teams, including representation from education, police, probation and social services.

1998: Early Years Development Partnerships established to integrate education and childcare at the local authority level following on from the White Paper, *Excellence in schools*, published in 1997, and the Green Paper, *Meeting the childcare challenge*, published in 1998.

1998: White Paper, *Meeting special educational needs: a programme of action*, required local authorities to improve agency collaboration to strengthen support for children with special needs.

1998: Launch of Quality Protects, requiring inter-agency collaboration to ensure that children in need gain maximum benefits from education opportunities, health and social care.

1999: Sure Start launched, involving joint working to improve services for pre-school children.

1999: Health Act established a statutory duty of partnership between NHS bodies and local authorities.

1999: Revised guidance on child protection issued, *Working together to safeguard children*.

2000: Publication of the shared *Framework for the assessment of children in need and their families*.

2000: Local Government Act placed on local authorities a requirement to prepare community strategies.

2001: Health and Social Care Act placed a duty of partnership on relevant agencies.

2001: Children's Fund launched to reduce social exclusion for children aged 5–13.

2001: Connexions service launched to provide universal careers and general support to young people aged 13–19 through multi-agency working and partnership with other agencies.

Scotland

In Scotland, since the early 1980s, many regional councils have developed inter-agency approaches such as Youth Strategies which aim to reduce the need for formal intervention in the lives of young people through a range of informal and non-statutory support.

1993: White Paper, *Scotland's children* published, in which collaboration is an important aspect.

1995: The Children (Scotland) Act placed a statutory duty on local authorities to produce children's services plans in consultation with health, housing agencies, voluntary organisations and representatives of the children's hearing system.

Recent history of partnership working

As the previous section has demonstrated, the need for better joining-up of policy and services has been a key theme running through recent policy developments in relation to children and young people. More generally, too, partnership working has been an important New Labour theme since the 1999 White Paper, *Modernising government* (Prime Minister and Minister for the Cabinet Office, 1999). Indeed,

Kelly (2000) argues that partnership is central to New Labour's agenda, is necessary to delivering its commitment to improve public services, and is linked to other New Labour concepts including active citizenship and democratic renewal. But the history of partnership working stretches back beyond current New Labour pre-occupations. Perri 6 traces partnership working, in the guise of inter-organisational co-ordination, back to the mid-nineteenth century (Perri 6 et al, 2002, pp10–11). Similarly, Pollitt describes attempts to co-ordinate policy-making and administration during the Churchill government of the 1950s (Pollitt, 2003, p36). Taylor (2000) discusses the history of joint working in relation to poverty and regeneration and demonstrates the long history of inter-agency relations between health and social services.

However, most commentators identify the Thatcher governments of the 1980s as a crucial phase in the recent history of partnership working (Whittington, 2003a; Perri 6 et al, 2002; Goss, 2001). In the period after the election of the first Thatcher government there was increasing concern about what were seen as spiralling costs within the public sector and inefficient use of resources. This was underpinned by a set of ideas that came to be known as the 'New Public Management' that had at its core the belief that the role of identifying needs for services and planning to meet those needs could be separated from the role of delivering the services. Running alongside these ideas was the New Right belief in the market as a more efficient and responsive provider of services than the public sector. These two strands of thought, which characterised Thatcherite thinking about the public sector, led to the policy of exposing what had been hitherto public sector services to competition. Consequently what had been multi-functional public sector organisations, such as local authorities, were now obliged to contract with a wide range of private and voluntary sector organisations.

During this period concerns about the public sector, together with an ideological predisposition against publicly provided services, led to fragmentation within the public sector along a number of different dimensions. Firstly, there was organisational proliferation as a result of the separation of purchasing and providing roles. Secondly, there was fragmentation arising from the increased number and type of organisation that might now be involved in planning and provision of services. Thirdly, there was further fragmentation as a result of the transfer of responsibility from multi-functional elected authorities (eg, local authorities) to a wide range of single-purpose bodies typically overseen by an appointed board.

However, while this process of organisational fragmentation was going on, there was also an increasing policy focus on a number of complex and intractable issues – 'wicked issues' such as social exclusion, community safety, the environment and regeneration. These issues were characterised by their 'cross-cutting' nature. In other words, they did not fall clearly within the remit of any one single organisation. Furthermore, they were seen to be beyond the ability of any single organisation working alone to solve. Instead a range of organisations with different perspectives, expertise and resources might conjointly be able to make some impression (see also Department of the Environment, Transport and the Regions, 1999). As a result the 1990s saw the development of multilateral partnerships involving the public, private and voluntary sectors, in part stimulated by the availability of central government funding, especially in relation to regeneration.

Richards presents this process in terms of three paradigms (DETR, 1999b). The first, covering the period from the Second World War until the 1980s was characterised by 'government joined up through policy consensus and the community of professional practice'. As the policy context changed this paradigm was replaced by another which was designed to achieve increased economy and efficiency in public spending, but in achieving these fragmented the system for delivering service outputs. Once some aspects of economic competitiveness had been achieved, this paradigm was also replaced, as is the case currently, by a new paradigm which focuses on the effectiveness of the outcomes of public policy and service. Thus the legacy of the second paradigm was a 'loss of local capacity to integrate across boundaries and the overloading of central integrating capacities' (DETR, 1999b, p7).

By the time of the election of the Labour government in 1997 the combination of a series of pressing policy issues, combined with the desire to modernise public services and a commitment to the 'Third Way' led to partnership arrangements becoming the instrument of choice across a wide range of policy areas including regeneration, health, community safety, teenage pregnancy, drugs and youth crime. There has, since 1997, been a veritable explosion of partnerships at local level together with a succession of central government initiatives intended to support and stimulate joint working. These include the setting up of the Regional Coordination Unit in 2000 with a remit to ensure better co-ordination of area-based initiatives and the establishment of a number of other new units within the Cabinet Office to improve policy-making and service delivery as follows.

- *The Prime Minister's Delivery Unit* – established to strengthen capacity in Whitehall to deliver government's key objectives.
- *Office of Public Services Reform* – established to strengthen the capacity of the public sector to deliver the government's key objectives and advise on reform of public services with a focus on changing the way in which policy is implemented including better joining up of services.
- *Public Service Agreements (PSAs)* – each sets out the aim of the department or policy, objectives and performance targets. To promote joint working there were initially three cross-cutting PSAs covering the criminal justice system, action against illegal drugs and Sure Starts for pre-school children with welfare to work added subsequently.
- *Public Services Productivity Panel* – advises on ways of improving the productivity and efficiency of departments. In May 2000 the panel published *Working in partnership* to assist local health communities involved in joint planning to implement systems to support the NHS's national information strategy (National Audit Office, 2001, pp23–24).

Partnership working, then, is not new. What is perhaps new is that the partnerships that have been developed since 1997 have increasing legitimacy, longevity and are broader in scope. Furthermore, the increasing preoccupation with the delivery of outcomes in relation to prescribed targets and the involvement of service users and citizens has upped the stakes in relation to partnership working; the demands that are being made on them have increased. They not only have to deliver challenging targets within specified timescales but they have to do so through inclusive structures and processes. Furthermore, there is increasing recognition that delivery of these outcomes is unlikely to be achieved in the short term and so long-term strategies are necessary. As a result a number of partnership bodies are acquiring an air of permanence. As Sullivan and Skelcher write:

> The imperative for achieving cross-cutting outcomes provides a longer term agenda for partnerships and encourages the articulation of joint outcomes to which all partners subscribe but which are not organisationally specific. (Sullivan and Skelcher, 2002, p21)

A further development that arises as a result of the proliferation of partnerships is the need to find some mechanism for linking partnerships to each other and to rationalise plans across partnerships. The work of the Social Exclusion Unit and in particular the *Joining it up locally* report of the Policy Action Team 17 (Department of the Environment, Transport and the Regions, 2000a) pointed to a proliferation of area-based initiatives and to the need to integrate their planning within a new framework of local strategic partnerships (LSPs) with a responsibility for local plan rationalisation. Proposals for LSPs were also taken forward in the local government modernisation programme through the community leadership role and the duty to prepare community strategies through a community planning process overseen by a LSP. (For a discussion of the progress of LSPs and their relationship to theories of urban governance, see Bailey, 2003.)

To sum up, partnership working is not new either in social care or in other areas of public policy. However, a number of factors have, over the last decade, come together to create increased pressure for partnership working. These can be summarised as: pressures created by the fragmentation of service planning and delivery systems that occurred as a result of the separation of purchaser and provider roles and the increasing number of organisations involved in service delivery; pressures created locally because of an increasing focus on outcomes; and pressures to resolve, creatively and collaboratively, apparently intractable and complex policy problems.

Scope of the publication

The overall aim of the Barnardo's 'What works?' series is to consider the question: what are the best ways to deliver the kinds of outcomes wanted by children and those who are responsible for their welfare? This 'What works?' publication is concerned with partnership working. More specifically it is concerned with strategic partnership working in localities in relation to services and interventions for children and young people.

The objectives of the publication are:

- to inform policy-makers, service planners, managers and practitioners of the best current evidence of effective approaches to service planning and provision by strategic partnerships
- to provide practical guidance to the above on how to plan, fund and deliver services in partnership for children and young people.

The emphasis throughout is to use evidence of 'what works' to uncover the best possible approaches to working in partnership, to draw conclusions and to present the information in a way that will be useful and relevant to policy-makers and service planners involved in managing, delivering and reviewing services for children and young people in a wide range of agencies operating in the statutory, voluntary and independent sectors.

The focus of this book is partnership working at the strategic level. This includes service planning and policy-making but excludes service delivery. The focus is also primarily on horizontal linkages rather than vertical joining up. However it is recognised that it is far from always the case that effective co-ordination exists between levels of government (see, for example, DETR, 1999). While joined-up government is one aim, essentially involving better co-ordination across government departments, our purpose is to look at the co-ordination of governance through partnerships that involve not only statutory sector organisations but also voluntary and community organisations and, in some cases, the private sector too.

In the next chapter we review the types of 'evidence' that have informed this publication. Chapter 3 considers definitions of partnership working and reviews a range of theories that underpin different models of, and approaches to, partnership working. Chapters 4 and 5 review the evidence relating to partnership processes. This material is organised around partnership formation and development (Chapter 4) and maintaining partnership momentum (Chapter 5), including involving children and young people and the broader community. Chapter 6 is centrally concerned with measuring progress towards outcomes and frameworks for evaluation, including a discussion of the criteria that might be appropriate for assessing the effectiveness of partnerships. In the final chapter conclusions are drawn.

2 What kinds of evidence help us to understand what works?

There are numerous publications on partnership working. This chapter reviews the types of literature that are helpful to us in trying to reach a view as to 'what works'. This report constitutes a review of the evidence in relation to partnership working; however, it is not a systematic review. This is not a matter of semantics. Systematic review refers to a particular technique for assessing *all* the relevant material and evaluating the strength of the evidence it contains. While this review of the evidence is wide-ranging we do not pretend that it is comprehensive. Similarly, while we have not included references to studies that are obviously flawed, much of the available literature has explored process rather than presenting empirical evidence on outcomes of partnership working. It has not therefore been feasible to exclude non-empirical studies, or studies that focus only on process issues – the issues of *how* we do strategic partnership working. We need to continue to strengthen the state of the evidence; Chapter 6 therefore addresses how we can shift to a more outcome-focused approach to researching and evaluating strategic partnerships.

Four different types of literature inform this review: official publications and guidance; research and evaluation reports; 'toolkits' and 'how to' guides; and theoretical syntheses and overviews. These four types of literature are reviewed in turn.

Official publications

The first group consists of official publications from a range of government departments and agencies including consultation papers, guidance documents and so on. These typically set out the requirements on agencies involved in specific policy areas of initiatives to work in partnership, identify the benefits of so doing and may provide guidance on the preferred form of partnership working to be adopted in particular contexts. While many of these documents are undoubtedly evidence-informed it is sometimes difficult to discern which have been informed by evidence and which are, to a greater extent, reflective of political priorities or pragmatic considerations.

For example, the Department of Health, Department for Education and Employment and Home Office's *Framework for the assessment of children in need and their families* (2000) provides guidance, underpinned by evidence-based knowledge, on developing a framework for assessing children in need and their families and describes how this is intended to contribute to integrated working. The Department of Health's (2002a) *Keys to partnership* provides good practice guidance on partner-ship development for agencies involved in planning and providing services for people with learning disabilities, in order to implement the vision set out in the government document, *Valuing people*.

Other examples include guidance on partnership working produced by the then Department for Education and Employment (DfEE) that draws out the lessons from the literature (Hutchinson and Campbell, 1998). The NHS Executive produced a good practice guide to working in partnership (NHS Executive, 2000) which uses a 'whole systems approach' to partnership working. The Department of Health, DfES, Home Office and the National Assembly for Wales have also produced guidance on inter-agency working to safeguard children (Department of Health et al, 1999).

A further group of publications within this category are inspectorate and inquiry reports. These are often particularly relevant because they identify issues relating to negative outcomes and/or failures of agencies to work in partnership from which lessons can be learned. Examples in this category include the Joint Chief Inspectors' report (2002) on *Safeguarding children*, the Social Services Inspectorate report (2002) on children's services and the Ofsted, Audit Commission and Social Services Inspec-torate report (2003) which examined the work of the first wave of Children's Fund partnerships.

Research and evaluation reports

This broad category of literature consists of reports of research and evaluation of two types. The first type is where research into, or evaluation of, partnerships was the primary purpose. The following are all examples of such reports.

- Roberts and colleagues (1995) set out to learn the lessons for partnership working through research into the experience of different kinds of partnerships in a range of English local authorities.
- Gaster and colleagues (1999) report on case study research examining the factors influencing relationships between local government and the voluntary sector. A 'governance' perspective is adopted which is underpinned by a belief

that the key issue for any local area is what the local needs and priorities are and how they can best be met by the range of agencies working in the area. The authors identify a number of different models of partnership working and conclude that which kind of partnership is set up depends on the purpose and aspirations of main players (see chapter 2 for models).

• Local Government Association (1999) reports on research to identify ingredients that have contributed to successful partnership working, barriers that still remain and what can be done to overcome them, arrangements for involving citizens and accountability and co-ordination of partnerships.

• Harding and colleagues (1998), in research for the then Department of Environment, Transport and the Regions, report on case studies of 18 regional or sub-regional partnerships. This research was designed to enhance the department's understanding of the factors underpinning successful partnerships and the way they contribute to strategic regeneration objectives.

• The then Department of Environment, Transport and the Regions (2000b) commissioned a mapping exercise of 11 local authorities examining perceptions on motivations for engaging in partnership arrangements, management arrangements and evaluation techniques.

• The Office for the Deputy Prime Minister and the Department of Transport (2003) commissioned a survey of all English local strategic partnerships which, among other things, identifies the issues that LSPs are grappling with as partnerships are developed.

• Roaf (2002) uses a detailed case study of inter-agency work on special educational needs to draw out the factors that contribute to or inhibit the development of effective inter-agency practice.

• Weinstein and colleagues (2003) bring together a series of papers which together contribute to the book's overall argument that collaboration between professionals and with service users and carers is essential to the successful delivery of care services. The aim of the book is to contribute to the development of effective collaborative relationships by offering analysis of collaboration and partnership, exploring their policy and practice contexts and sharing evidence and examples of good practice.

• Pettit (2003) examines the effectiveness of joint working between community adolescent mental health services and schools and identifies ways in which this might be improved in a research report commissioned by DfES using a survey and case studies.

- Hamer and Smithies (2002) describe 16 case studies of integrated planning across local strategic partnerships with a focus on the links between community strategies and health improvement and modernisation plans. On the basis of these case studies key issues for more integrated planning and delivery of services are identified and ideas for local, regional and national action proposed.
- Dean and colleagues (1999) undertook research for Scottish Homes, reviewing the effectiveness of the partnerships in which it was involved. A case study approach was used and the focus was very much on the processes of partnership working.
- Atkinson and colleagues (2002) and Wilson and Pirie (2000) both report on major studies identifying factors contributing to the success of multi-agency working.
- Frye and Webb (2002) conducted research into a wide variety of different partnership types in order to draw conclusions about the key factors responsible for making partnerships successful.
- *Joining up to improve public services*, produced by the National Audit Office (2001), is a detailed review of five 'joint working' initiatives from which are drawn more general conclusions about what is needed for successful joint working.
- Carley and colleagues (2000) investigated urban regeneration partnerships in England, Wales and Scotland and drew conclusions on factors contributing to more effective partnership working.

In the second category of research, partnerships are not the main or the only focus but the research or evaluation findings nevertheless comment on, or have implications for, partnership working. Examples are as follows.

- *Cross-cutting issues in public policy and public services* (DETR, 1999a) aims to provide detailed advice to central and local government on the successes and failures of approaches to designing, implementing and reviewing policies and specific initiatives for tackling cross-cutting issues. It adopts a whole-systems perspective, focusing not only on ways in which issues are dealt with at local government level, but also the development and handling of policy in relation to these cross-cutting issues in central government. It includes studies of a small number of specific cases which illustrate successes, or failure, in addressing issues in a holistic, outcome-oriented way.

- In Russell and colleagues' evaluation of City Challenge (1996), research and evaluation questions relating to partnership working were included among others.
- Webb and Vulliamy (2001) present the evaluation of a three-year Home Office funded project involving placing social-work trained home–school support in secondary schools to support pupils at risk of exclusion, with the aim of reducing the number of exclusions from school and to ensure a cohesive local authority response. In the course of this evaluation 'useful lessons were learned about developing cooperative working at operational level' (Webb and Vulliamy, 2001, p316).
- The Scottish Office's Central Research Unit (Scottish Office, 1996) commissioned an evaluation of the urban partnerships responsible for the comprehensive regeneration of large peripheral housing estates – Castlemilk in Glasgow, Wester Hailes in Edinburgh, Ferguslie Park in Paisley and Whitfield in Dundee. The evaluation in each area identifies the extent to which objectives have been met as well as examining the ways in which the partnerships have developed.

Toolkits and guides

The third type of literature consists of 'toolkits' and 'how to' guides intended to provide accessible advice on partnership working. The Health Development Agency (Markwell, 2003) has published a comprehensive guide to the resources available to support partnership working. Guides and toolkits in turn fall into two categories: those that are research-based and those that are based on practice experience.

Research-based guides include the following.

- The Civic Trust (1999) has published a useful and comprehensive guide to working with cross-sectoral regeneration partnerships for voluntary and community groups.
- The Audit Commission (1998a) has produced a guide based on fieldwork with 14 different partnerships and a wide array of individuals and also an account of initiatives to improve joint working in local government based on a review of their own local government audits.
- Thorlby and Hutchinson (2002) have produced a 'sourcebook' for the New Opportunities Fund drawing on established good practice, academic research

and new research, consisting of 12 case studies of current partnerships. Aimed explicitly at practitioners, the guide seeks to present the 'realities of partnership working', opportunities that can arise through partnership working, things that can go wrong and what works in practice (Thorlby and Hutchinson, 2002, p2).
- The Scottish Executive's Effective Interventions Unit (2002) identifies the key principles of partnership working based on case study examples of how partnership works in practice in employability provision for drug users.
- The Scottish Executive (2002) has also published a guide to improving inter-agency working based on the experiences of three local health care co-operative pilot projects designed to improve local services and utilising an organisation development approach.

Examples of guides that draw on practice and experience rather than research include the following.

- Leeds Health Action Zone have produced a guide and self-assessment tool (Frearson, 2002).
- The Health Development Agency's *The working partnership* (2003a, b and c) is a guide and self-assessment manual that draws on both evidence about partnership working and the experience of those who contributed to its production. The tool was tested in community planning partnerships in Scotland and at 15 pilot sites across Europe.
- Wilson and Charlton (1997) is a cross-sectoral guide to partnership working.
- Campbell and Percy-Smith (2000) produced a guide for the Department for Education and Employment to inform the setting up of learning partnerships based on a review of the literature and practical experience.
- Harrison and colleagues (2003) drew on the authors' experiences of studying and working in various partnerships. It makes extensive use of 'case studies' which are described, somewhat idiosyncratically, as 'fictitious adaptations or extensions of the authors' experiences'.

Toolkits and guides of the kind reviewed here are increasingly available electronically through a range of websites relating to partnership working and related topics. (A good example is the set of toolkits available under the generic heading of 'Build a partnership' on the renewal.net website.) The most useful of these resources are listed in the Resources section at the end of the book.

Theoretical overviews and syntheses

The final category consists of more theoretical and, typically, academic works that tend to try to account for the development of partnership working as a phenomenon and/or provide theories and models that are intended to help us to understand partnership working better. This group of studies of partnership working consists of overviews and syntheses which are used to generate more generalised discussion of issues in relation to partnership working including categorisation of theories, models and approaches. Much of the more theoretical academic writing is pitched at such a high level of abstraction that it is sometimes difficult to discern its relevance to practitioners and policy-makers. However, some of this literature is used to inform the next chapter on theories and models. For example, Sullivan and Skelcher (2002) investigate the place of collaborative activity in the achievement of public purpose. Its prime focus is on collaboration that occurs beyond the centre – that takes effect at regional, local and neighbourhood levels. Glendinning, Powell and Rummery (2002) examine the place of partnerships in New Labour thinking and in particular whether the partnerships advocated and created by New Labour 'represent a new and distinctive form of welfare governance' (p1). Ranade and Hudson (2004) explore the conceptual issues informing different forms of inter-agency collaboration.

Other issues

While the main focus of this book is strategic partnership working for children and young people, there are important lessons that can be learned from the experiences of partnership working in other contexts and sectors. For that reason we draw on literature from across sectors and organisations although wherever possible we provide examples and illustrations that relate to partnership working for children and young people.

Most of the descriptive and evaluative literature relating to partnerships is heavily skewed towards process – how partnerships operate – rather than outcomes – what happened as a result of partnership working. While there are some notable exceptions which are discussed in Chapter 6, this emphasis in the literature needs to be appreciated. Thus it is probably possible on the basis of the 'evidence' to set out what works in terms of partnership processes; however, it is much more difficult to make any definitive statements about whether and what kinds of partnerships result in certain kinds of outcomes. There is such a pervasive assumption within current policy and practice that partnership working is 'a good thing' that there is very little examination of whether that is indeed the case. As a result the emphasis is very much on ensuring that partnerships work effectively rather than on evaluating the underlying assumption that they produce better outcomes than would otherwise have been the case. This issue is returned to in Chapter 6.

Finally, it is worth mentioning that there is an extensive literature focusing specifically on public-private initiatives. This literature has not been included as it relates primarily to economic development and the Private Finance Initiative and is, currently, of limited relevance to strategic partnership working for children and young people.

3 **Definitions and models**

Despite the profile given to the concept of partnership within policy there is little agreement over what partnerships actually mean or what they should look like. There are a range of different approaches to partnership working, underpinned to a greater or lesser extent by different models and theories.

A review of the evidence in relation to partnership working necessarily involves some preliminary work on definitions. We need to be able to define what a partnership is (and what it is not) and to be able to distinguish partnerships from other related concepts, structures and ways of working. In practice, coming up with a neat definition of partnership is not easy, as I shall show in the next section. However, while there is no single definition that commands universal acceptance there is at least fairly widespread consensus on what the key elements of partnerships and partnership working are or ought to be.

One of the factors contributing to difficulties over definition is the fact that partnerships can be defined either in terms of structures – what kind of a structure or organisation is a partnership or ought to be; ways of working – the kinds of decision-making and other processes associated with partnerships; or a set of ideals to be aspired to even if not achieved in practice (Hutchinson and Campbell, 1998, p8). So we can think about partnerships in terms of organisational forms, ways of working or theoretical models or some combination of all three. For example, a report for the Department of the Environment, Transport and the Regions defines partnership working in the local authority context in the following terms:

> A local authority partnership is a process in which a local authority works together with partners to achieve better outcomes for the local community as measured by the needs of the local stakeholders and involves bringing together or making better use of resources. (Department of the Environment, Transport and the Regions, 2000b, p1)

This working together requires the development of a commitment to a shared agenda, effective leadership, a respect for the needs of the partners, and a plan for the contributions and benefits of all the partners.

The dynamic aspect of the process requires specific goals of partnership working to be identified, performance to be evaluated, and the assessment of the continuing fit between partnership activities and community needs and priorities.

Any working definition of 'partnership' is likely to be informed – explicitly or implicitly – by a set of assumptions or ideas – theories that determine the parameters of what we are talking about. A key purpose of this chapter is to review approaches to partnership working, the models to which they give rise and the theories and assumptions that inform or underpin them.

One key assumption underpinning all models of partnership working is that there are benefits that accrue as a result of partnership working; the literature suggests a wide range of both benefits and also potential costs or risks. These costs and benefits are summarised in the final section of this chapter.

Definitions

A number of writers refer to the difficulties of defining partnerships or partnership working (see, for example, Powell and Glendinning, 2002, pp2–4; Audit Commission, 1998, p16; Roberts et al, 1995; Hutchinson and Campbell, 1998). Indeed, at times it almost seems to mean whatever anyone wants it to mean:

> Partnership means many things to many people. Indeed often it is not clearly defined precisely because its ambiguity can be politically attractive. It is difficult to be opposed to partnership. (Roberts et al, 1995, p6)

Part of the difficulty arises from the relationship of partnership to a wide range of related terms and concepts that can be (although often mistakenly) used interchangeably with 'partnership'. The related terms and concepts uncovered during the literature review can be found in Box B together with definitions that attempt to delineate each of them; overlap still exists and is probably inevitable but this review does perhaps help to identify what partnership is not. Less clear are those terms which refer to concepts that partnership might be considered a sub-set of or contributor to. Thus it could be argued that partnership working is one way of potentially 'joining up' governance and/or policy; that it constitutes a particular form of 'collaboration'; that it contributes to 'holistic governance' and can facilitate 'multi/cross-agency working' and 'co-ordination' of services.

Perri 6 and colleagues do not use the word 'partnership' but nevertheless identify a spectrum of possible relationships in relation to integration as follows:

- *taking into account* – strategy development considers the impact of/on other entities
- *dialogue* – exchange of information between entities
- *joint project* – temporary joint planning or joint working between entities
- *joint venture* – long-term joint planning or joint working between entities
- *satellite* – separate entity created to serve as an integrative mechanism between existing entities
- *strategic alliance* – long-term joint planning and working between entities on issues core to the mission of at least one of them
- *union* – formal administrative unification of entities maintaining some distinct identities
- *merger* – fusion of entities to create a new structure with a single new identity (Perri 6 et al, 1999, p63).

Partnership working would probably fit somewhere between 'joint project' and 'union' but falling short of outright 'merger' on this spectrum.

BOX B

Terms related to 'partnership'

- **Holistic government/governance:** Integration and co-ordination at all levels and in relation to all aspects of policy-related activity – policy-making, regulation, service provision and scrutiny; mutually reinforcing means and objectives (see in particular, Perri 6 et al, 2002).
- **Joined up:** Deliberate and co-ordinated planning and working which takes account of different policies and varying agency practice and values. This can refer to thinking or to practice or policy development.
- **Joint working:** Professionals from more than one agency working directly together on a project.
- **Multi-agency/cross-agency working:** More than one agency working together; services are provided by agencies acting in concert and drawing on pooled resources or a pooled budget, eg, youth offending teams.

- **Multi-professional/multi-disciplinary working:** Working together of staff with different professional backgrounds and training.
- **Inter-agency working:** More than one agency working together in a planned and formal way.
- **Cross-boundary working:** Agencies working together on areas that extend beyond the scope of any one agency.
- **Cross-cutting:** Cross-cutting issues are those that are not the 'property' of a single organisation or agency. Examples include: social inclusion, improving health, urban regeneration.
- **Integration:** Agencies working together within a single, often new, organisational structure.
- **Networks:** Informal contact and communication between individuals or agencies.
- **Collaborative working/collaboration:** Agencies working together in a wide variety of different ways to pursue a common goal while also pursuing their own organisational goals (but see Sullivan and Skelcher, 2002, p14, for a somewhat different specification).
- **Co-operation:** Informal relationships between organisations designed to ensure that organisations can pursue their own goals more effectively.
- **Co-ordination:** More formal mechanisms to ensure that organisations take account of each other's strategies and activities in their own planning.

A review of the definitions of partnership used in the literature shows that they can refer predominantly to organisational forms or structures; decision-making processes or modes of governance; and desired outcomes or some combination of all three. For example, the following definitions focus on *process* as a means of achieving specific *outcomes*:

> A process in which two or more organisations or groups work together to achieve a common goal, and do so in such a way that they achieve more effective outcomes than by working separately. (Thorlby and Hutchinson, 2002, p8)

> The mechanisms used by two or more organisations or individuals to work together on a shared agenda while keeping their own organisational or individual identity and purpose. (Arc, 2002, p9)

By contrast, Harding and colleagues (1998, p16) focus on the nature of organisational relationships in this definition:

> Formalised bodies established by two or more autonomous partners, none of whom is simply under contract to another, with the purpose of attaining substantive or symbolic goals that no partner could achieve independently.

The following two definitions emphasise collective and purposive endeavour:

> A partnership is a group of stakeholders brought together from a range of organisations, to be responsible for tackling mainly long term challenges and opportunities in which they have a shared interest. (Frye and Webb, 2002, p4)

> A coalition of organisations and individuals who agree to work together for a common aim, or a set of compatible aims ... Members of a partnership share resources and responsibilities and agree to work together in a cooperative and mutually supportive fashion. (Civic Trust, 1999, p4)

Finally, the Audit Commission's definition comes closest to covering all of these aspects. Here partnership working is defined as:

> A joint working arrangement where the partners:
> - are otherwise independent bodies
> - agree to co-operate to achieve a common goal
> - create a new organisational structure of process to achieve this goal
> - plan and implement a joint programme
> - share relevant information, risks and rewards. (Audit Commission, 1998a, p8)

The common elements across these and other definitions can be summed up as follows.

- The structure and/or way of working involves two or more organisations.
  - These organisations retain their own separate identities (ie, this is not 'integration').
  - The relationship between the organisations is not that of contractor-provider.
- There is some kind of an agreement between the organisations to work together in pursuit of an agreed aim.

- This aim may be shared or negotiated (ie, common or compatible, see Civic Trust, 1999, p4).
- This aim could not/is unlikely to be achieved by any one organisation working alone (ie, the partnership gives rise to some additional benefit or 'collaborative advantage', see Huxham, 1996).
- Relationships between organisations are to a greater or lesser extent formalised (ie, it is more than a 'network') and expressed through an organisational structure and the planning, implementation and review of an agreed programme of work.

Types of partnership

The consensual elements within the definition of partnership can nevertheless accommodate a wide variety of different *types* of partnership. Dimensions along which partnerships can vary and which provide the basis for categorisations are as follows:

- sectors involved – public, private, voluntary, community; all sectors may be represented or all partners may come from just one sector
- partnership purposes – what is the partnership seeking to do; the focus may be on a single issue or more broadly based; strategic or operational
- structure – corporate or non-corporate; advisory or executive
- level – spatial area covered, eg, neighbourhood, area, sub-region, region
- size – small or large number of partners
- scale – significant resources at their disposal or very few
- representation – who is involved; key actors; partnership may include community or user group representatives or may be composed entirely of 'professionals'
- actual and potential impact (Thorlby and Hutchinson, 2002; Audit Commission, 1998a).

The Civic Trust (1999) classifies partnerships into five basic types on the basis of their underlying purpose.

- *Strategic partnership* – often involving most senior people in the key local agencies. Focus on strategy rather than the running of programmes.
- *Service co-ordination partnership* – set up when major agencies decide that co-

ordination will lead to greater impact and efficiency of services. 'In these types of partnership, each partner goes away to run its own services, but gets together periodically with the other partners to discuss how they can co-operate.'

- *Themed partnership* – eg, partnerships working on a particular subject or theme. 'In these types of partnership, the agencies involved set up joint programmes or seek funds to link a number of separate programmes together in a much more integrated way.'
- *The neighbourhood regeneration partnership* – area-based partnerships. 'These partnerships are usually multi-functional and set up programmes to improve the area on a number of fronts simultaneously.'
- *The local trust* – some partnerships are set up with the intention of becoming a permanent fixture; they usually have to develop an asset base to generate income in the future. 'Some local trusts are owned by the local community, or are voluntary groups. Others are run as partnerships with representatives from all sectors on their boards, contributing to the work of the trust.'
(Civic Trust, 1999, pp11–12)

In addition, there is the possibility of hybrid models involving more than one of the above purposes.

In a similar vein, Gaster and colleagues identify a 'ladder of partnership' as follows.

- *Information exchange:* involving mutual learning, knowledge of what each partner does and could do. Openness about decision-making processes. New methods of access to information (including IT).
- *Planning action:* involving identifying local and service needs where cross-boundary working is needed and could be effective. Debate (and agree) local needs and priorities. Agree different partners' contributions, decide actions and processes. Identify (the need for) new partners.
- *Implementing projects and service plans:* joint or separately taken action on agreed plan; identify monitoring methods and review processes; mutual feedback on 'success/failure'.
- *Co-ordination and co-operation in practice:* involving active co-ordination process; co-ordinator knows what's going on, draws on each (autonomous) partner as appropriate, helps to nurture developmental and co-operative culture and involve and support new partners.
- *Collaboration and full partnership:* involving separate and distinct roles but

shared values and agenda. Pooled resources, blurred boundaries, continuously developing to meet changing needs. Less powerful partners supported to play a full role.

(Gaster et al, 1999, p9)

Richards categorises partnership activity in terms of the kinds of problems to which increased co-ordination is seen as the answer. The first of these are the classic 'wicked issues', complex and often intractable social problems that do not fall within the remit of any single organisation. The second are what she refers to as 'tame problems' – those where solutions are known or where there is a chance of finding an answer. Some of these issues may require co-ordination because they are on the boundaries between organisations and are likely to require the deployment of a diverse knowledge and skills base. In this case Richards suggests that the form of co-ordination required will have the following features:

- an ambitious national strategy developed by national government with a structured programme for its delivery including objectives, targets, performance management
- cross-sector leadership capacity to focus attention on results
- flexible/pooled budgets allowing money to be spent in ways that partners think will lead to the desired results
- evaluation and learning from processes of experimentation.
  (DETR, 1999b)

The third category relates to services that are well-established but which could now be delivered in a more joined-up way as a result of technological change. In this case the purpose of the partnership would be to link up a range of currently separate services around other principles (eg, life episodes, client groups) than function.

Perhaps the most commonly made distinction is between strategic and operational partnerships (see, for example, Scottish Executive, 2002, pp8–9). The former typically has responsibility for planning, co-ordinating and commissioning services while the latter has responsibility for managing and delivering a particular set of services. (As indicated in Chapter 1, the main focus for this publication is strategic partnerships.)

A related distinction is between executive and advisory partnerships. Executive partnerships directly contract with organisations, agencies and individuals to provide works and services needed for the purposes of the partners or are able to act in some other way on behalf of partners. They may be corporate bodies, able to enter into contracts and employ staff or, if not, these functions are delegated to one of the partners to undertake them on behalf of the partnership. Advisory partnerships do not usually commission or procure services. Rather, partners agree collectively what each should then do individually to further the collective objectives of the partnership. Most are not corporate bodies.

The National Audit Office (2001) distinguishes between formal and informal partnerships. The former entails agreement by the partner organisations to rules for working together through contract, protocol or framework agreement. Informal partnerships, by contrast, entail organisations working together through liaison, consultation or unwritten mutual agreement. Both of these types of partnership are distinguished from what the National Audit Office refers to as the 'realignment of organisational boundaries' which entails the bringing together of the whole or parts of two or more organisations to create a new organisation.

The 'informal partnership' in the National Audit Office's categorisation is probably closer in form to a 'network' as defined by Sullivan and Skelcher. They regard informal relationships between players as networks whereas partnerships are 'formalised relationships that are less than complete integration' (Sullivan and Skelcher, 2002, p42). However, they go on to say that some networks can become 'semi-formal' and take on an organisational form while not all partnerships are formalised. They conclude that 'partnerships are perhaps a particular form of networking'.

The Audit Commission (1998a) proposes four possible models of partnership working categorised by organisational form. The advantages and disadvantages of each are identified (see Box C). Consideration of the various possible models leads them to conclude that all partnerships require at least one body (board or steering group) that is recognised as the mechanism for decision-making: 'A properly constructed partnership board is essential to make sure that the partnership delivers its objectives and remains accountable to the partners' (Audit Commission, 1998, p19).

BOX C

Models of partnership working

1. Separate organisation

A distinct organisation set up with a separate legal identity, this model is suitable for larger partnerships with a medium- to long-term life span that need to employ staff. This model has the advantages of: providing a clear, strong identity for the partnership; as a separate entity it may be able to do things that individual partners cannot; reducing the likelihood of any one partner dominating; employing staff who identify with the partnership rather than an individual partner agency. A disadvantage is that the formal commitments required to set it up may be off-putting to smaller organisations. There is a risk that partner agencies may become distant from the partnership if it takes on too much of a life of its own.

2. 'Virtual' organisation

The partnership has a separate identity but a distinct legal identity is not created. The partnership can have its own name, logo, premises and staff. However, at a formal level one partner employs staff and manages resources. This model avoids some of the complex issues that need to be addressed if setting up a legal organisation while, at the same time, having a distinct partnership identity. However, responsibilities and accountability may be unclear.

3. Co-locating staff from partner organisations

This is a less formal arrangement involving groups of staff from partner agencies working together to a common agenda under the direction of a steering group. There may be pooling of resources but staff continue to be managed by their employing agency. This model can be appropriate for partnerships that do not require a strong, separate identity and can work well where there are high levels of trust enabling an informal arrangement to work. However, it is generally not suitable for major new projects and can lead to staff having confused loyalties.

> ### 4. Steering group without dedicated staff resources
>
> This is the simplest and least formal model. The partnership consists of a steering group without dedicated staff or budget so outputs must be capable of being implemented through partners' mainstream programmes and staff. This model may be effective where the am is to improve co-ordination of services; it is not suitable for major new initiatives or partnerships with a longer timespan.
>
> Source: Audit Commission, 1998a, pp17–19

Harding and colleagues describe an alternative basis for categorising partnerships depending on the main drivers for partnership working. Three 'ideal types' of partnership are proposed. The first are termed 'shotgun partnerships' because they are the products of compulsion. Typically they offer access to additional resources in return for partnership working. The second are termed 'defensive partnerships' and are described as 'conservative reactions to institutional changes through which local agencies attempt to retain well-established service delivery roles for themselves in a policy environment in which they are no longer the sole players'. In other words they are a pragmatic response on the part of certain agencies to the changing policy environment. The final type are 'offensive partnerships' described as 'bottom up attempts to get to grips with issues that have become too complex to be amenable to single agency, market-based or public policy-dominated approaches' (Harding et al, 1998, p11). Although these three approaches are conceptually distinct the authors argue that they can co-exist within a single organisation.

Whichever form of categorisation is adopted it should also be remembered that partnerships can evolve and change as their purpose changes, contexts alter and relationships evolve. Lowndes and Skelcher suggest that partnerships go through a 'life-cycle' involving changes at each stage (1998, p320). So typically at the 'pre-partnership' stage the form of collaboration is 'characterised by a network mode of governance based upon informality, trust and a sense of common purpose'. As the partnership becomes established and consolidates its activities the form of collaboration is 'characterised by hierarchy based on assertion of status and authority differentials and the fomalisation of procedures'. The programme delivery phase is 'characterised by market (or quasi-market) mechanisms of tendering and contract, with low levels of cooperation between providers'. Finally, as the partnership enters the termination or succession phase, there is a 're-assertion of a network governance mode as a means to maintain agency commitment, community involvement and staff employment'.

While this particular conceptualisation of a partnership life-cycle may not fit all cases of partnership working, it nevertheless does alert us to the notion of dynamism within partnerships as they move from formation to delivery and then to closure or succession. It also highlights the need to keep the partnership under review in terms of its structure, processes and ways of working to ensure that they are still 'fit for purpose'. The Audit Commission (1998a) also adopts a partnership life-cycle approach identifying likely problems at each stage and proposing ways of overcoming them. In this publication the need to review and possibly restructure the partnership to take account of evolving roles is also noted (see also Chapter 5).

Theories of partnership working

There have been a number of different attempts to theorise partnership working. For example, Sullivan and Skelcher identify three sets of theories or approaches to collaboration which relate to wider underpinning theories. These are termed 'optimist', 'pessimist' and 'realist'. 'For optimists collaboration takes place in order that a shared vision may be achieved.' Furthermore, the optimist perspective is characterised by two underpinning theories: 'that collaboration will result in positive outcomes or improvements for the system as a whole' and 'that the stakeholders share a level of altruism in relation to collaboration, that is, that future positive outcomes for the system override the desire for sectional gain by the participating organisations' (Sullivan and Skelcher, 2002, p37).

The pessimist perspective is characterised by an underpinning belief that 'collaboration takes place in order that stakeholders may preserve or enhance their power, prioritising personal or organisational gain above all else' (Sullivan and Skelcher, 2002, p39).

The realist perspective is informed by the belief that 'it is the wider environment – or more specifically changes in the prevailing contest – that are critical in determining the incidence of collaboration' (Sullivan and Skelcher, 2002, p41).

In an earlier publication Lowndes and Skelcher (1998) argue that the way in which interactions between organisations are conceptualised broadly relates to two organising principles: competition and collaboration. Thus 'resource-dependency' theory is centrally concerned with the way in which scarce resources are fought over by competing organisations on the basis of their relative power and domination. This rather crude model is developed into a more sophisticated version in 'network theory' through the inclusion of norms and values and their role in sustaining relationships between organisations over time (Lowndes and Skelcher, 1998, pp316–317). By contrast, collaboration theory is underpinned by the idea of 'synergistic gain' or 'collaborative advantage'. In other words by sharing resources, risks and rewards organisations can generate benefits that could not be achieved through other means (Lowndes and Skelcher, 1998, p317). However, operating within 'resource-constrained environments' can lead to difficulties for collaborative arrangements; in reality relationships are rarely either exclusively collaborative or exclusively competitive. As a result Lowndes and Skelcher suggest that the notion of 'governance' may provide an alternative basis for understanding partnerships. They distinguish between:

- a *market* mode of governance revolving around contractual relationships which set limits on the possibilities for collaboration and co-ordination
- a *hierarchical* mode of governance in which co-ordination is secured by 'administrative fiat' but at the possible cost of a reduction in flexibility and innovation
- a *network* mode of governance where actors identify complementary interests and develop inter-dependent relationships based on mutual trust, loyalty and reciprocity which then enable collaborative activities to be developed (Lowndes and Skelcher, 1998, p319).

Much of the literature on modes of governance suggests a chronological development from hierarchy in the period prior to the 1980s, markets in the 1980s and early 1990s and networks in the period since the 1990s. However, as Ranade and Hudson note this is to over simplify. 'Rather than superseding each other as the dominant "operating mode" of government, markets, hierarchy and networks have been *overlaid* on each other and *co-exist* in complex sets of relationships in different settings' (Ranade and Hudson, 2004, p36). Lowndes and Skelcher also argue that different organisational arrangements can co-exist with different modes of governance and, indeed, the latter is likely to change as the partnership moves from formation through delivery to closure or succession (Lowndes and Skelcher, 1998, p320).

Holistic governance is the broadest of the family of terms identified above in Box B. It refers to integration of policy, agency and function across and between tiers of governance, and across sector in order to address the 'wicked issues' and in recognition that people have 'joined-up problems'. Perri 6 and colleagues define holistic governance as '... working back from a clear and mutually reinforcing set of objectives to identify a set of instruments which have the same happy relationship to one another' (Perri 6 et al, 2002, p32). Holistic governance is seen by the authors to necessitate, but go beyond, 'joining up' or 'co-ordination'. As such, partnership working is, or could be, one manifestation of holistic governance.

Benefits and costs of partnership working

Whichever model or theory of partnership working is employed, they all contain the underlying or explicit assumption that partnership working is 'a good thing', that it will give rise to wide-ranging benefits that could not, or are unlikely to, accrue in the absence of the partnership.

The first set of assumed benefits is the elimination of contradictions or tensions between policies, programmes or interventions (Pollitt, 2003, p35; Perri 6 et al, 2002). This will result in more efficient deployment of resources (Hutchinson and Campbell, 1998; National Audit Office, 2001, p2; Health Development Agency, 2003a, p4) through the elimination of duplication, sharing of overheads, securing better value for money and achievement of economies of scale (Pollitt, 2003, p35; Arc, 2002, p15).

Secondly, partnerships are argued for on the basis that they result in more effective services as a result of clearer identification of service gaps (Arc, 2002, p15); improved integration and the overcoming of fragmentation (Audit Commission, 1998a, p12); involvement of the community and service-users and the harnessing of resources of individual partners (financial resources, skills, information, political access and people) (Lowndes et al, 1997, pp334–335). Furthermore, partnerships should result in services that are more integrated from the point of view of citizens or service users (Pollitt, 2003, p35; Local Government Association, 1999, p6; National Audit Office, 2001, p2; Health Development Agency, 2003a, p4; Audit Commission, 1998a , p9).

Partnerships may also build capacity to resolve policy problems, either through providing access to additional resources through grant regimes or leverage (Audit Commission, 1998a, p12; Harrison et al, 2003, p1), or through improving the flow of ideas and co-operation between stakeholders leading to greater 'synergy' or smarter ways of working (Pollitt, 2003, p35; Hutchinson and Campbell, 1998; Health Development Agency, 2003a, p4; Harrison et al, 2003, p1) and facilitating integrated approaches to complex, multi-dimensional and multi-agency problems (Audit Commission, 1998a, p11).

Where partnerships work well, there can be benefits in terms of increased understanding and trust between agencies. This, in turn, can lead to a greater willingness to take risks (Harrison et al, 2003, p1), enhanced potential for innovation and improved outcomes (Arc, 2002, p15; National Audit Office, 2001, p2).

So, to sum up, the working assumption throughout much of the literature is that partnership working results in benefits for service users, partner agencies and, to the extent that more effective outcomes are generated, society as a whole.

While partnerships are assumed to produce benefits, it is also recognised that there are costs associated with partnership working (see, for example, Glendinning et al, 2002; Hudson and Hardy, 2002; Wilkinson and Craig, 2002). These include higher financial costs because of delays and higher transaction costs (Ranade and Hudson, 2004, p47; Pollitt, 2003, p38). Furthermore, additional resources are rarely provided to support partnership working (Hogg, 2000, p16) and as a result many agencies struggle to meet the demands placed on them as a consequence of the proliferation of partnerships at local level. The costs of partnership working may also be unequally shared with those in the voluntary and community sector, who are often least able to bear them, suffering as a consequence (Ranade and Hudson, 2004, p47).

Pollitt (2003, p38) argues that the risk of failure is higher with partnership working because of increased complexity, the potential for irreconcilable difficulties between partners and lack of clarity in relation to accountability arrangements (see also Cabinet Office, 2000 and Harrison et al, 2003, p1). Complexity can also mean that it is difficult to effectively measure or evaluate effectiveness and impact (Cabinet Office, 2000).

Partnership working should generate more open and inclusive processes; however, there is also the risk of elitism and the exclusion of those who do not share the dominant view (Hutchinson and Campbell, 1998). Similarly, partnership working is dependent on trust between partners. If this is absent it can lead to unwillingness on the part of individual partners to give up resources or influence and the avoidance of difficult issues around which it is difficult to generate consensus (Harrison et al, 2003, p1).

Conclusion

This chapter has demonstrated that just as there is no single definition of partnership working so also there is no single model or approach. As Goss writes:

> Despite the multiplicity of models in development, there is not, as yet, any clarity to the language or any agreed definitional precision ... There are no unique models of successful partnership, nor is there any easy route to the design of the successful partnership. (Goss, 2001, p101)

However, despite this lack of clarity there is widespread commitment to the idea of partnership working and enthusiasm as to the benefits that it can bring. Overall the prize to be won from partnership working is what Huxham (1996) refers to as 'collaborative advantage'. This occurs when 'something unusually creative is produced ... that no organisation could have produced on its own and when each organisation, through collaboration, is able to achieve its own objectives better than it could alone' (Huxham, 1996, p37). The remaining chapters are concerned with what the evidence tells us about how to maximise the chances of collaborative advantage being secured while at the same time minimising the risks.

4 Getting started

There are numerous guides to partnership working, and research and evaluation reports that draw lessons on how to 'do' partnership working effectively (see Chapter 2). Fortunately, almost without exception, they agree on the main stages in developing a partnership and the factors that help or hinder this process. The aim of this chapter is to synthesise the lessons from across this literature that relate to the formation and early stages of development of partnership working. We begin by examining the processes involved in taking the initial decision to set up a partnership before moving on to look at the early development phase and the key tasks that will have to be undertaken including defining the partnership's purpose, vision and approach. The development of the partnership group – membership, leadership, structure and organisation – is then examined followed by the less tangible aspects such as building a team and developing collaborative ways of working. Finally we examine what is needed to turn the vision into a workable strategy.

While the literature suggests that all these elements are necessary to the process of developing a partnership, it is important not to see the development phase as a linear process during which the various elements identified above are pursued sequentially. In most cases timescales for partnership development do not, in any case, allow this. Rather we should see the elements within the overall process of partnership development as a series of circles that overlap in terms of both time and activity. For example, the building of effective team working within the partnership may be an outcome from the process of developing a purpose and vision (see Figure 1). Dean and colleagues write:

> ... good constructive relationships would develop organically and as a by-product of simply working together. Thus, whilst there was agreement that more explicit effort towards team-building would be beneficial for the development of partnerships, there was also a view that teams were built unconsciously through taking action and delivering outcomes as well as through conscious efforts. (Dean et al, 1999, p13)

Agreeing to work in partnership

Partnerships may be developed 'bottom-up' in response to a specific need or issue

Figure 1 **Partnership building**

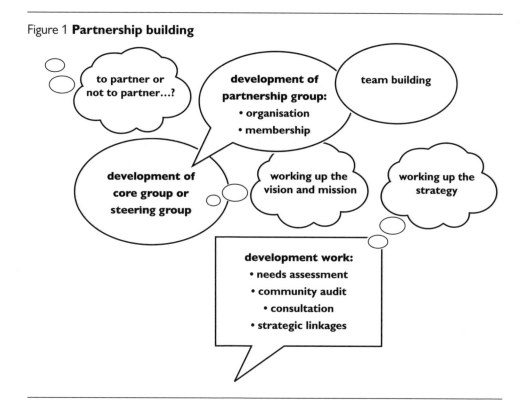

that has been identified locally and that lends itself to a partnership approach. This is more likely to be the case in relation to delivery of services than the strategic level. At the strategic level the 'need' for partnership working tends to be identified 'top-down' by central government as a means of pursuing a specific policy goal or set of goals. Hudson and Hardy identify acknowledgement of the need for a partnership as an important 'partnership principle'. This is likely to be a product of two variables: the extent to which there is a history of partnership working and the extent to which there is a recognition of the need to work in partnership (Hudson and Hardy, 2002, p53; see also Department of Health, 2002a, p14).

Wherever the idea for partnership came from originally it is important to ask the questions: is forming a partnership the best way of achieving the desired outcome? what is the added value that a partnership can bring? (see Box D).

BOX D

What is the added value?
Two plus two equals how many?

2 + 2 = 3   overlap, duplication, waste; competition not partnership

2 + 2 = 4   co-ordination, co-operation and collaboration produce efficient working

3 + 1 = 4   not so good; more of what one partner wants, less what the other wants; unequal power, no overall difference

2 + 2 = 5   synergy; joint working produces more effective working between partner organisations

2 + 2 = 6   synergy plus leverage, as joint working generates extra special funding for the neighbourhood from a third party

2 + 2 = 7   synergy plus leverage plus main programme bending, as the big organisations adjust their own programmes

2 + 2 = 8   synergy plus leverage plus mainstreaming plus influence, as partnerships influence national policy.

Source: www.renewal.net, 2002

If the answer to these questions is that a partnership approach is needed, or indeed, if government prescription removes the element of choice, then the next question to ask is: is it necessary to set up a *new* partnership or is there an existing partnership structure that could be adapted for the purpose? Partnership development, as this chapter will show, can be a time-consuming process. The time involved in setting up a new partnership should, therefore, be weighed in the balance against the timescale available for the achievement of the outcomes specified for the programme or partnership. As Frye and Webb note:

> As effective partnerships can take several years to develop, new partnerships are inappropriate vehicles for outcomes expected in the short to medium terms. New partnerships should only be set up when the nature of the problem requires them, and there are

genuine prospects of creating the conditions for success within the desired time frame. If the 'centre' wants short term results, another method of delivery or an existing partnership should be used instead. (Frye and Webb, 2002, p11)

It may be possible to make minor adjustments to the scope or membership of an existing partnership so that it can take on responsibility for the new programme, strategy or function. Such an approach is more likely to deliver results quickly than developing a new partnership from scratch. 'Existing partnerships can achieve big wins quickly at lower costs' (Frye and Webb, 2002, p11). Using an existing partnership can also result in additional gains of relevance to the overall goal (see Box E). However, the National Audit Office warns against using an existing arrangement solely because it is believed to be cheaper and easier.

BOX E

A new partnership?

'When the Department for Education and Skills were considering how to implement its national childcare strategy it identified that it could expand the role of the existing Early Years Development Partnerships to include childcare. This was a more efficient use of local resources and also improved the integration of early education with childcare.'

Source: National Audit Office, 2001, p52

Partnership development phase

If the decision is taken that a new partnership is necessary then we enter into what might be called the 'partnership development phase' during which a number of important tasks will need to be carried out in order to get the partnership up and running. To oversee this phase it will almost certainly be necessary to set up a working group, task group or steering group. In setting up this group proper consideration should be given to the nature of the work that must be carried out and, therefore, who needs to be involved. Since the steering group is likely to become the core of the eventual partnership it is important that the 'right' organisations are involved from the start while, at the same time, avoiding the development of closed groups or cliques. The steering group will also need to be appropriately resourced so that it is able to undertake the development work effectively. The resources required will include:

- human resources – someone who is able to undertake the activities associated with the partnership development phase
- information – access to research, intelligence and data
- financial resources – to purchase research support, if necessary; to undertake consultation activities, etc
- office – including office equipment and support
- time – this is often in short supply; the timescales for undertaking the development work associated with centrally prescribed partnership formation are often very short.

Development tasks

The development phase typically involves certain key tasks. These are important because they will underpin and inform the development of the vision and strategy. Failure to undertake these tasks effectively may result in a strategy that does not relate to local needs, is unconnected to other programmes and initiatives and does not reflect stakeholders' priorities or concerns. All of these tasks will involve a combination of research, data analysis, discussion and negotiation. Depending on the resources and skills available to the steering group it may be necessary to buy in specialist external assistance for some of these tasks.

An analysis of needs may be an important first step in determining what the goals and objectives for the partnership should be. It can also provide a baseline against which subsequent progress can be measured (Health Development Agency, 2003b, p14). The other side of needs is existing services and provision. The local needs analysis should include an audit of existing provision so that the relationship between needs and provision can be examined, and service gaps or duplication identified. Related to this is the issue of other local and national initiatives which are working in the same area or with the same target groups. The development phase should identify such initiatives, develop linkages with them, including ongoing means for communication, so that synergy is maximised (National Audit Office, 2001, p52).

While some programmes and initiatives are quite prescriptive in terms of their scope, identifying in some detail the target groups, populations or geographical areas, others will require at least some degree of local scoping. This might involve specifying geo-graphical boundaries or neighbourhoods within which intervention is to take place, or the characteristics of target groups within the population:

> There are often no clear geographical boundaries to neighbourhoods; no-one agrees where a neighbourhood begins or ends. But local partnerships must know the area they are expected to cover, and what are the boundaries between their areas of responsibility and someone else's. (www.renewal.net, 2002, p4)

The National Audit Office recommends making geographical boundaries as far as possible co-terminous with existing administrative boundaries in order to simplify relationships and liaisons with other bodies (2001, p52).

Consultation on needs, issues and priorities is an important part of the partnership development phase. Consultation can play a number of different roles. It can raise awareness of the programme and partnership; it provides opportunities to listen to a wide range of views that should inform the development of the eventual strategy; and it can create ownership of the programme. Consultation may need to take place with key stakeholders and partners or potential partners; within the key agencies involved in developing the partnership; with service users or those likely to be directly affected by the programme; and with the wider community (Campbell and Percy-Smith, 2000, p4). It is not possible in this publication to provide detailed advice on how to carry out effective consultations; however, there are a number of guides to the process available (see the Resources section, p123).

Developing the vision and mission
Once this work has been undertaken the steering group is then in a position to develop its vision (what it is trying to achieve) and its mission (how the vision is to be achieved), including the general approach to be adopted and the principles that should inform the approach. Throughout the literature the importance of agreeing a shared vision is emphasised (see, for example, Frearson, 2002, p4; Thorlby and Hutchinson, 2002, p31; National Audit Office, 2001, p47; Hutchinson and Campbell, 1998, p40; Hudson and Hardy, 2002, pp54–56; Roxburgh and Arend, 2003, p31). The vision statement is important because it is this that defines the part-nership's purpose. As such it should, ideally, be 'inspirational' (Thorlby and Hutchin-son, 2002, p31); agreed and understood by all partners (Scottish Executive, 2002, p8); and be based on jointly held values (Hudson and Hardy, 2002, p55).

Developing a vision that all partners can sign up to will require partners to make explicit what 'success' looks like for them individually, and clarify what a *shared* vision of success looks like (Health Development Agency, 2003b, p14). This in turn is likely to require openness about partners' respective interests and mutual respect between them (Health Development Agency, 2003b, p6). The process of developing the vision may, therefore, be easier if members of the steering group have already built up good working relations (see 'Building the team' section below).

While the vision sets out *what* the partnership is trying to achieve, the mission statement should set out *how* the vision is to be achieved. In practice, however, the two terms are often used interchangeably. Together the vision and mission statement should provide a reference point for subsequent decisions.

Developing the partnership group

Governance structure
One aspect of deciding the approach to be used to achieve the vision is to decide on the type of partnership that is going to be developed. A governance structure needs to be agreed for the partnership that facilitates efficient and effective decision-making and is consistent with the vision and approach that the partnership is taking. In some cases the form of partnership is specified in government or programme guidance; in other cases a greater degree of local discretion is permitted. It should also be recognised that different stages in the development of the partnership may require different models of organisation. For example, in its evaluation of partnerships involved in the 'Right Fit' initiative, Arc identified the following models of organisation at different stages in the partnerships' development:

- pre-partnership collaboration: lead organisation bids, then invites others to join or use existing partnership or partnership formed around bid writing
- partnership creation: involving a core of partners but with good communication between them – limited network governance; peripheral partners having been consulted would be engaged during programme delivery
- delivery: core partners maintain network governance; others move to more hierarchical form of governance; others use a mixture of network and hierarchical (Arc Research and Consultancy Ltd, 2002, pp21–23).

This is consistent with the study of modes of governance and organisational

arrangements undertaken by Lowndes and Skelcher (1998) which sees organisational development in terms of partnership life-cycles (see Chapter 3). Thus the need to
'get things done' is likely to lead to greater formalisation and the setting up of organisational structures with clear, roles, responsibilities and accounting mechanisms
(Lowndes and Skelcher, 1998, p324).

The question then is what kind of organisational structure is appropriate? One way
of thinking about types of organisational structure is to think about the nature of the
relationships between partners. Hutchinson and Campbell (1998, pp31–33) suggest
that there are two main types. The first is a federation where the partnership acts as
a management organisation for a network of organisations which cede power and
influence to the partnership in order to achieve certain agreed goals. Federations are
typically developed where there is a relatively large number of organisations
involved, each with their own goals and interests. The second type is a 'hub network'.
Here one out of a number of organisations takes on the role of lead partner and co-
ordinates and integrates the activities of all the others.

Some funding regimes *require* the identification of a lead partner who is (at least)
responsible for financial accountability. But the role of lead partner may also entail a
range of other functions including:

- convenor of meetings
- home of partnership secretariat
- external liaison with policy-makers, funders
- accountable body
- champion of the partnership.

If a lead partner is required it is important that their role and remit is clearly delin-
eated so that they do not come to dominate the partnership's agenda (Thorlby and
Hutchinson, 2002, p28).

The National Audit Office argues that there is no 'one size fits all' for joint working
arrangements (National Audit Office, 2001, p52). The precise legal framework that
is necessary is likely to depend on what the partnership needs to do as a partnership.
For example, it may have to be established as a legal entity if it needs to own property
or enter into contracts in its own right (see Box F). Whatever governance arrangements are adopted they need to be clear so that partners understand their roles,
responsibilities and liabilities. And, most importantly, the organisational structure

should follow, rather than drive, partnership activity (Campbell and Percy-Smith, 2000, p4). Box G provides details of the range of different partnership arrangements that have been set up to manage the Children's Fund.

BOX F

Organisational form

'Some Sure Start partnerships have become companies limited by guarantee, with a board of directors, to enable them to contract for services whilst other partnerships have decided not to incorporate because they wish to preserve their flexibility to adapt their partnership arrangements to new circumstances which may develop.'

Source: National Audit Office, 2001, p52

BOX G

Children's Fund partnership arrangements

Independen:t Separate, stand-alone local Children's Fund partnership structures. These partnerships have infra-structures that are created and maintained specifically to develop and manage the activity of the local Children's Fund.

Integrated: Partnerships that report to, and are sub-groups of, existing strategic partnership structures, such as LSP and Children and Young People's Strategic partnerships.

Networked: Partnerships that have originated in, and grown from, pre-existing partnership arrangements, but have developed dedicated structures and a separate identity.

Developmental: Following a review process that identified difficulties or significant local change, the original partnership has been decommissioned and new arrangements are being built.

Cross-initiative: The partnership builds on and works alongside the partnership arrangements that have been created for other allied initiatives, in particular On Track and Sure Start.

Multi-layered: A complex structure that has a number of levels, including a central board/steering group and community or locality based sub-groups, with various reporting mechanisms into and links with other partnership groups.

Foundational: The original Children's Fund partnership has acted as the driver and base for other strategic and developmental partnerships to grow, for example, Pathfinder Children's Trusts and arrangements for IRT.

Source: Morris and Spicer, 2003, p17

Membership

Once the type of partnership has been agreed decisions then need to be taken on the size of the partnership, which organisations should be represented and which individuals from within those organisations would be the most appropriate to represent them. It may be the case that until this point partners have been involved in a relatively ad hoc way – including those who have turned up to early meetings to discuss the initiative or taken on development roles. However, at some point during the development phase a decision will have to be taken on the nature and composition of the partnership in the future. There are two aspects to this process: selecting the right organisations and selecting the right individuals to represent those organisations.

Some partners may be mandatory or certain core partners may be obvious because of the nature of the programme or initiative. However, there will still be choices to be made about who else to involve and, from within a sector or interest group, which organisations to involve (Audit Commission, 1998a, p20). The key considerations here are likely to be:

• striking a balance between involving all organisations or groups that have an interest or a role to play and the need to deliver the partnership's objectives as efficiently as possible. Very large partnerships may be inclusive but they can also be unwieldy and difficult to manage and motivate (National Audit Office,

2001, p52; Hutchinson and Campbell, 1998, p25). (See Box H and Chapter 5 for other ways of involving interested organisations.)

- the need to involve organisations within whose remit the objectives or goals of the partnership are perceived to lie. As partnerships increasingly take on responsibility for tackling cross-cutting issues and seek to do this in a holistic way, so there is a tendency for the number of organisations who could potentially be involved to increase.
- categories of organisations who might need to be involved, including funders or potential funders; statutory providers; community and voluntary groups; expert groups and advisory organisations; and groups/organisations likely to be affected by the outcomes of the initiative (Thorlby and Hutchinson, 2002, p12).
- the possible roles that organisations might play in relation to the partnership including key decision-makers, consultees and informed parties (see Box H).

BOX H

Deciding who to involve

Thorlby and Hutchinson (2002) suggest the application of the Power-Interest matrix (below) to help decide what role stakeholders might play in relation to the partnership. 'Power' relates to how much influence an organisation can bring to the partnership. 'Interest' relates to how much of a stake an organisation has in the outcomes bein worked towards.

		INTEREST	
		LOW	HIGH
POWER	LOW	A. Non-partners	B. Keep informed
	HIGH	C. Consultees	D. Key decision makers

Source: Thorlby and Hutchinson, 2002, p11

Not all potential partner organisations may be willing to come on board, especially those who are suffering 'partnership fatigue' due to their representation on numerous partnership bodies. It may, therefore, be helpful to consider the incentives for partnership working in any particular case. The overarching incentive is, perhaps, a sense of shared ownership of the partnership and its goals. However, it might also be necessary to demonstrate to potential partners that there is 'something in it for them' (Scottish Executive, 2002, p8).

The National Audit Office suggests the following possible incentives.

- Promoting action through leadership: 'Strong leadership can be an important incentive particularly if this convinces joint working participants of the high priority and commitment behind the initiative.'
- Ensuring that objectives have direct relevance to partner organisations: 'The better the fit between the objectives of the initiative and those of organisations involved in the partnership the easier it becomes to join up. This means ensuring that objectives are defined in a way that is relevant and meaningful to participating organisations.'
- Providing financial incentives: 'Additional funds can be a powerful incentive to work together.'
- Allowing partnerships greater flexibility in their use of resources: 'An alternative way of incentivising organisations to work together is to give them greater control over how they use their resources. In 2001, 20 local authorities agreed to pilot local Public Service Agreements. In return for greater freedom, for example the ability to borrow money or to disapply government regulations and administrative procedures – such as freedom to keep revenue raised from fines or to switch grants between different programmes – local authorities have committed themselves to achieving a range of performance targets which address both local and national priorities' (National Audit Office, 2001, p53; see also Hutchinson and Campbell, 1998, pp30–31).

However, the National Audit Office also warns (rather enigmatically) that 'Incentives do not always have the impact originally intended' (2001, p53).

Individual organisations that are invited to join a partnership will also need to consider whether it is appropriate for them to become involved. This may require an assessment of how far the partnership contributes to their own organisational purpose or mission, what additional benefit that organisation might bring to the partnership, the likely costs in terms of time as well as money and the possible risks involved. Small community and voluntary organisations will need to be especially cautious about their involvement in partnerships. Typically they operate with few resources, especially human resources, and therefore often find it difficult to take on roles over and above those that are central to their own organisational purposes (see Chapter 5 for a further discussion on supporting the involvement of community and voluntary organisations).

Having identified the organisations and secured their commitment to join the partnership, the next step is to identify the right individuals within the organisation. As Frye and Webb note: 'The most important features of an effective partnership are engaging the right people and ensuring they function as a genuine team' (Frye and Webb, 2002, p6). In thinking about who the individual members might be, the aim should be to achieve a 'balance' within the overall team. Thus there is a need for leaders, creative thinkers, problem-solvers and those who can resolve conflicts. More generally it is important that the partnership includes senior people from the partner organisations who have the authority to take decisions on behalf of their organisations. Dean and colleagues (1999, pp60–61) identify the following dimensions of 'appropriateness':

- seniority of individuals, ie, a representative with sufficient decision-taking powers or delegated authority
- the need for parity in the perceived seniority of representatives from different organisations
- partners' capacity to ensure continuity of representation over time.

There is, within the literature, the notion of partnerships as dynamic organisations whose needs change as they develop. For example, the Audit Commission states that: '... new partnerships need champions with the charisma, authority and negotiating skills to get the show on the road. These champions are often not the right people to lead the partnership throughout its life, but they have a vital galvanising role in the early days' (Audit Commission, 1998a, p20). The need to review partnership structures, membership and terms of reference is discussed further in Chapter 5.

Management arrangements
Having arrived at an organisational structure and agreed membership, decisions will need to be taken as to what kinds of management arrangements are necessary so that

the business of the partnership is transacted as efficiently as possible. Again it is important to stress the need to retain some flexibility in the arrangements so that they can be changed as the partnership develops. Hudson and Hardy identify the 'establishment of clear and robust partnership arrangements' as one of their six 'partnership principles'. It refers to the need to ensure that 'partnership working is not hindered by unduly cumbersome, elaborate and time-consuming working arrangements' which, they claim, will sap partners' enthusiasm and commitment (Hudson and Hardy, 2002, p59).

In deciding what kinds of organisational and management arrangements are appropriate, the cost of resourcing them should also be considered. Some programmes specify a percentage of the total programme budget that can be spent on management and administration. However, the National Audit Office reminds us that: 'In funding joint working arrangements there are additional or increased support services likely to be needed including administrative and secretarial support, financial management, premises for meetings, attendance allowances to cover for staff absence at meetings and training for partners' (2001, p55; see also Wilkinson and Craig, 2002, p37; Scottish Executive, 2002, p8; and the various accounts in Glendinning et al, 2002).

It may be helpful to think about the management arrangements in terms of a series of functions that will need to be fulfilled or jobs that have to be done. These are:

- strategic planning and decision-making
- discussion, listening to advice and/or expert opinions
- operational management
- reporting; accountability; monitoring.

There is widespread agreement that partnerships need some kind of executive board that undertakes strategic planning and decision-making, monitors and reviews progress and is generally responsible for driving the partnership's programme forward. How big should the executive board be? It needs to be large enough to be inclusive but small enough to be efficient. It could consist of the entire partnership or a smaller core group. If the latter option is selected then consideration will need to be given to the role of the wider partnership group. Does this group have a formal role? If so what is it and what is the relationship between this group and the executive?

Meetings of the executive board will, typically, work through a set agenda and will be predominantly focused on 'business'. However, there will also be a need for wider, more free-ranging discussion to take place on specific issues or to explore possibilities prior to a formal decision being taken. This discussion may involve the whole board and could be carried out at pre-defined discussion slots in the regular agenda, or through specially convened meetings or away-days. Such meetings can also serve the additional purpose of allowing board members to get to know each other better and to build up trust (see section on 'Building the team', p54). In addition to, or instead of, such sessions involving the whole board, there may also be a role for sub-groups, working groups or task groups. These may be composed only of smaller numbers of board members or may have the power to co-opt other people who have specialist knowledge or skills of relevance to the group's remit. Such groups may be standing groups that meet regularly for the duration of the partnership, or they may be short-life groups that are set up to undertake a particular task or set of tasks. Either way it is very important that any such group that is set up works to agreed terms of reference covering:

- remit
- membership
- delegated powers
- reporting arrangements.

In addition the partnership may feel that it needs regular recourse to a wider group of stakeholders who, while they do not need to be involved in decision-making, should be informed about and consulted on the work of the partnership on a regular basis. This might lead to the setting up of an advisory group or consultative forum. Again it is important that terms of reference are agreed for such a group including clarification of issues relating to the group's status, how it reports, where it gets its information from and who is responsible for convening, servicing and chairing the group (Thorlby and Hutchinson, 2002, pp27–28).

A partnership might be involved in the 'hands on' or operational management of the partnership's work. However, more typically, this function is undertaken by a programme manager or co-ordinator who – either alone or with a staff team – is responsible for overseeing the development and implementation of the strategic plan devised by the partnership board. This is likely to involve the day-to-day management, co-ordination and monitoring of partnership activities, contracting with delivery organisations, operating financial systems, managing staff and compiling reports for the executive and/or other stakeholders.

The developing partnership will very quickly need to develop processes and procedures that allow business to be transacted smoothly and efficiently:

> Partnership processes are 'engines' for delivery of strategy and actions. They have to satisfy the needs of a variety of interested parties: community groups, government departments, auditors, partner organisations, elected officials. So they need proper management, which includes performance checks against expectations, and appropriate adjustments to maintain sustainable and effective performance. (Health Development Agency, 2003b, p10)

This will entail, at a minimum:

- clear structures and procedures for the efficient organisation of meetings, including chairing and recording business and decisions
- systems for managing and accounting for income and expenditure
- systems for collecting monitoring information and compiling reports
- human resource management including recruitment, payroll and staff development and training.

Leadership

Effective leadership emerges from the literature as an important critical success factor for partnership working (see, for example, National Audit Office, 2001, p49; Scottish Executive, 2002, p8; Hutchinson and Campbell, 1998, p46; Health Development Agency, 2003b, p6; Roxburgh and Arend, 2003, p32). Partnership activity can be complex, involving multiple players and challenging objectives. Effective leadership should operate in such a way as to keep the partnership on track and working towards the agreed goal. However, leadership does not necessarily reside in a single individual. Indeed leadership needs to be effective at a number of different levels. Firstly, at the strategic level, the chair of the partnership needs to be active in holding the programme together while at the same time ensuring that partners continue to work collaboratively. However, other members of the partnership will also take on leadership roles both in relation to specific areas of work, eg, chairing sub-groups or working groups, and also by acting as champions for the partnership within their own agencies. Effective leadership also needs to be evident in relation to the management of the programme. This role may be undertaken by a member of the partnership board or, more typically, by a programme manager or co-ordinator who is employed for that purpose.

The skills required for leadership include:

* facilitation – especially the ability to secure the involvement and commitment of a wide range of organisations in discussion and decision-making
* influencing and communication – such as the ability to convince partners and a range of stakeholders of the purpose of the initiative and what it can achieve and that there are no hidden agendas: 'Partners should demonstrate commitment by acting as role models and motivators' (Health Development Agency, 2003b, p6).
* organisation and planning – to co-ordinate a range of partners and activities to achieving a common goal (National Audit Office, 2001, p49; see also Health Development Agency, 2003b, p6; Harrison et al, 2003, p24).

Building the team

An effective partnership is more than just a collection of members, organisational structures and processes and procedures. It is also a set of complex relationships between individuals and organisations. The literature refers time after time to the need for inter-personal and inter-organisational relations based on trust, openness and honesty (see, for example, Civic Trust, 1999; Goss, 2001; Hudson and Hardy, 2002; Lowndes and Skelcher, 1998; Stoney et al, 2002; Sullivan and Skelcher, 2002; Roxburgh and Arend, 2003, p32). If there is a history of effective partnership and inter-agency relations in the locality then it may be the case that such relations already exist. If not, then relationships need to be built. The costs of failing to do so can be high, as the 2002 Joint Chief Inspectors' report on safeguarding children notes:

> … in areas where there were long-standing tensions between agencies and less co-operation, it was difficult to achieve the necessary level of inter-agency commitment to ensure that arrangements to safeguard children were effective. (Joint Chief Inspectors, 2002, p4)

The partnership 'team' consists of both members of the partnership board and also employed staff (and, in some cases, volunteers) who are responsible for delivering the strategy. In the early stages of partnership development it is unlikely that a full staff team will have been appointed. Therefore the processes associated with 'building the team' should not be seen as a one-off exercise but as ongoing work which will need to be revisited throughout the life of the partnership (see also Chapter 5).

Building the partnership team involves the following elements to a greater or lesser extent depending on the history of partnership working. The Department of Health's *Keys to partnership* (2002a) also provides a useful checklist of questions that partnerships and partners should ask (see Box I).

Getting to know each other: There is evidence from a number of studies (eg, Frearson, 2002, p4) that partnership working is more effective where partners already know each other and have good inter-personal relations. This may be easier to achieve where there is a history of partnership working or in a small geographical area. Where this is not the case time may need to be invested in 'team-building' activities (see, for example, Harrison et al, 2003, p29).

Improving understanding of each other's organisations: A number of studies have identified lack of mutual understanding of partners' organisations as a barrier to effective partnership working (see, for example, Lowndes and Skelcher, 1998, p323; Scottish Executive, 2002, p13). Time should therefore be invested in discussing each partner's organisational agendas, issues, priorities and the constraints that they are working within as well as challenging the stereotypes that individuals may have about each other's organisations. This process should assist the development of openness and trust between partners.

Building trust: Trust is frequently cited as a critical success factor in building partnership effectiveness (see, for example, Scottish Executive, 2002, p8; Lowndes and Skelcher, 1998). As Frye and Webb note: 'Before people are prepared to implement the partnership's decision in their own organisations, they need a high level of trust in each other and hence confidence in the collective decisions they take' (2002, p6). Furthermore, building trust is not a one-off task; it is 'hard won and easily lost, which means that the maintenance of trust is an endless and reciprocal task' (Hudson and Hardy, 2002, p57).

Developing mutual respect: For partnerships to work effectively there needs to be an atmosphere of mutual respect between partners. Improved understanding of each other's organisations should help develop mutual respect. However, it might also be necessary to agree a code of conduct for partnership meetings to ensure that individuals behave in an appropriate manner towards each other. 'The ability to work collaboratively and take collective responsibility for decisions reached is vital for effective partnership working. This requires that everyone's view is respected, and included in transparent and open discussion' (Frye and Webb, 2002, p7; see also Hudson and Hardy, 2002, pp57–58; Harrison et al, 2003, p29).

Equality and inclusivity: While the literature frequently mentions the need for equality between and inclusivity of partners (see, for example, Hudson and Hardy, 2002, pp57–58), there is also recognition that, in reality, not all partners are equal in terms either of the resources that they bring to the table or in terms of their power and influence. This issue is discussed in greater detail in the next chapter in relation to community and voluntary organisations. However, the following quote from a publication produced by the Local Government Association highlights some of the difficulties and tensions:

> All partnerships should try to avoid suggestions of dominance by one or other partner… Successful partnership working depends on a true partnership of peers in order to gain real commitment from all involved … all partners cannot be equal: some have statutory duties or responsibilities, others are taking risks … There can be senior and junior partners. Such partnerships can be made to work, provided roles are understood and accepted from the outset. The expectation of equality can become a barrier to good partnership working when it is inappropriate and unexplained. (Local Government Association, 1999, p11)

Support for new partners: Not all members of the partnership will come with experience of partnership working or substantive knowledge of issues relating to the partnership's objectives or the technical skills necessary to be an effective partner. Partners will therefore require training, development and support to help them develop their skills and knowledge. Not all partners will require the same level of input. However, at least some of the training and development sessions ought to involve all partners as there is considerable evidence to show (see, for example, Joint Chief Inspectors, 2002, p32) that shared training can help to overcome mistrust and misconceptions between partners. (The issue of capacity building is discussed at greater length in the next chapter.)

Commitment to and ownership of the partnership: Individual partners need to be personally committed to the partnership but they also need to be in a position to engender commitment and ownership at all levels, including senior levels, within their own organisation (see Hardy, Hudson and Waddington, 2000; Audit Commission, 1998a; Tomlinson, 2003, p8). Hudson and Hardy emphasise the importance of building commitment to the partnership throughout partner organisations including at operational level:

> The research evidence suggests that an organisational commitment to partnership working is more likely to be sustained where there is individual commitment to the venture from the most senior levels of the respective organisations. Without this it is possible that the efforts of partnership enthusiasts holding middle and lower-level positions will become marginalised and perceived as unrelated to the 'real' core business of each separate agency. (Hudson and Hardy, 2002, p56)

This may also entail addressing concerns about the implications of partnership working on the part of operational staff (Tomlinson, 2003, p8).

Conflict resolution: Partnerships bring together individuals and organisations with their own agendas and priorities. There is, therefore, always the potential for conflicts. These need to be confronted early on and mechanisms developed for their resolution. Resolving conflict successfully can help build trust and confidence (Frye and Webb, 2002, p6).

More generally the importance of establishing good working relations is stressed by the National Audit Office:

> If organisations do not establish good working relationships based on mutual support and trust and open sharing of information then joint working will fail and improvements in public services will not be achieved. (National Audit Office, 2001, p49)

However, at the same time it is recognised that this may not be easy to achieve because of the difficulties for individual partners of trying to balance the objectives and priorities of the partnership with those of their own organisation and of working in new and different ways involving the sharing of responsibility and authority.

BOX 1

Building the team: checklist of questions for partners/partnerships

Do we share the same values and aspirations?
- There is a common vision that is set down and interpreted in similar ways between stakeholders.
- The full range of stakeholders has been involved through effective planning process-es in developing this vision.

Do we have agreed priorities for significant policy and service shifts?
- Is there a common interpretation of where and how services are currently suc-ceeding and failing to meet people's needs and wishes?
- Is there agreement over the significant service changes that the partnership is designed to help achieve?
- Are the necessary links in place with other planning processes such as LSPs (Local Strategic Plans) and HIMPS (Health Improvement Plans) to ensure policy and service changes are linked to the mainstream?
- Have you established outcome criteria to show you whether changes have led to positive outcomes for people?

Is there a shared willingness to explore new service options?
- Are partners willing to open up all aspects of service and practice to scrutiny through approaches such as Best Value and user-led quality reviews?
- Is there a culture of innovation and positive risk-taking in terms of service planning and design?

Is there agreement about the boundaries of the partnership?
- Are resources aligned with administrative/geographical boundaries so that they can be shared flexibly?
- Are boundaries with other services agreed and clear?

Are we clear and comfortable with who will be responsible for what within the partnership?
- Is it clear where commissioning responsibility rests?
- Is there a common definition and understanding of commissioning?

- Is there a shared understanding of the nature of person-centred planning, care management and assessment and of who is responsible for which aspects?
- Is the nature of the relationship between commissioners and providers of services mutually acceptable?
- Is the role of service users in decision-making clear and acceptable to all?

Is there confidence that each party's resource commitment is clear and open?
- Each party is confident and accepts that the resources committed to the partnership fully reflect the partners' contributions in reality.
- Arguments over past financial issues have been put behind you.
- Financial systems are robust enough to monitor and track resource commitments.

Is there effective, committed leadership to the partnership vision?
- Key senior players understand the issues and implications around partnership and are committed to its development.
- Senior officers are able and willing to make the time and space to build partnership working into their organisational agendas.
- Key practitioners are committed to a multi-professional way of working.

Are there people with the time and capacity to take forward the partnership agenda?
- One or more individuals have been given a clear brief to lead on partnership development.
- Partnership is an integral part of everyone's work and job description.

Is there trust, openness and good will between key players?
- Key players at all levels in all organisations are able and willing to work together constructively.
- There are strategies in place for managing and addressing difficult relationships.
- Time and opportunity is being built into working practices to allow people to get to know and understand each other's agendas.

Source: Department of Health, 2002a, pp17–19

Developing the strategy

The partnership's vision and mission will need to be translated into a clear, comprehensive and detailed strategy that is owned by all stakeholders, informed by consultations, audits and the needs analysis and linked to other strategies, pro-grammes and initiatives (National Audit Office, 2001, p47; see also Health Devel-opment Agency, 2003b, p13). The strategy is important because 'if objectives are unclear or not shared, partners may work towards different, incompatible goals and fail to achieve desired outcomes' (National Audit Office, 2001, p47; see also Hutchinson and Campbell, 1998, p40; Hudson and Hardy, 2002, p55).

The strategy should consist of:

- a re-statement of the vision, mission, approach and principles
- a statement of aims and objectives – based on strategic choices; informed by central prescriptions but reinterpreted in the light of local circumstances
- rationale in terms of:
  - the partnership's understanding of local needs, issues and priorities
  - understanding of the national, regional and local policy environment and strategic linkages
- outcomes linked to objectives
- interventions to achieve the outcomes specified and informed by evidence of what works
- resources – financial, human, skills, information
- interim steps and milestones
- monitoring and evaluation plan.

The strategy will need to be set within an agreed time-frame which may be pre-scribed by a government department or may be decided locally by the partnership. The development of the strategy may require further consultation with partners and other stakeholders as options are considered and appraised.

Resources
Ensuring that sufficient and appropriate resources are available to deliver the partner-ship's objectives is an important parameter within which the partnership must work:

> Without sufficient resources, including appropriate skills, a joint working initiative will not achieve its intended benefits or these will not be capable of being sustained in the longer term; and value for money and propriety may be put at risk. Shortages of resources may result in staff having to 'fire fight' a variety of problems at the expense of the core objective of the joint working initiative. (National Audit Office, 2001, p48)

Typically partnerships are tackling long-term issues although their funding may be short-term. This creates particular challenges for partnerships:

> Funding for partnerships needs to be pursuant to the task. Partnerships need long-term funding in order to deal with long-term issues. Funding for partnerships also needs to be simple to access and, where possible, be delivered by a single strand of government. (Frye and Webb, 2002, p7)

The resources available to the partnership are likely to be varied in kind and to derive from different sources as follows.

- Financial resources – money – including the budget allocated to the partnership from central or local government. Typically this will come with 'strings' attached relating to when and on what it can be spent. Financial resources may also be available to the partnership via additional grants from other sources or from virement of partners' mainstream budgets.
- Human resources – people and their skills and knowledge including those directly employed by the partnership; secondees from partner organisations; officer time within partner organisations; and volunteers.
- Information available from publicly available sources and as a result of the research and intelligence-gathering activities of the partnership.

Partnerships need to manage their resources efficiently and effectively but they also need to be creative in their consideration and use of the resources available to them. As the Health Development Agency observes:

> Partnership working should create linkages, shared ways of operating, and connections between people at different organisational levels. It should also create tangible resources through economies of scale, and avoid duplicated effort through the sharing of physical assets or resources. (2003b, p20)

The way in which funding is provided to partnerships can influence how successful they are. The National Audit Office argues that central government should consider balancing the partnership's need for flexibility in the way its money can be used and the need of the central unit (or department responsible for control) to ensure that spending is targeted towards national priorities (National Audit Office, 2001, p55). Financing of partnership working typically takes one of two forms – pooled and ring-fenced budgets. The advantages and disadvantages of each are shown in Box J. The National Audit Office concludes: 'In general it is better for joint working for the partnership to have control over its funds. Pooled budgets allow greater flexibility, make it easier for partnerships to design solutions that fit local circumstances and encourage partnerships to develop a strategic approach. Separate ring-fenced budgets, especially combined with short-term or annual bidding for funds, militate against this' (2001, p55).

BOX J

Advantages of pooled and ring-fenced budgets

Pooled budgets: Funds which can be used to finance a range of activities are provided by a number of departments, agencies and local authorities.

Advantages
- Partners have greater flexibility in the way in which they can use funds.
- Partners can design solutions which fit local circumstances.
- Joint working is promoted because a number of organisations have an interest in how their money is spent.
- Accountability can be promoted by defining the outcomes to be achieved (with the partnership having discretion as to how they are achieved) and having measures to monitor progress.

Ring-fenced budget: Funds are designated by the sponsoring department for a clearly defined purpose and cannot be used for anything else without the prior agreement of the department.

Advantages
- Partners have to focus on achieving a specific objective often within a designated time period.
- Sponsoring departments have much greater control over how money is used.
- Clearly specified amounts of money are allocated to priorities with guaranteed funding often for a number of years.
- There are clear lines of accountability because responsibility for expenditure is clearly specified.

Source: National Audit Office, 2001, p55

Frye and Webb emphasise the importance of releasing funds to partnerships gradually and at a pace that allows them time to build up spending programmes:

> In some cases too much funding is offered to partnerships before they are operating effectively. This can distort the process of partnership working, such that it becomes dominated by 'spending money'. Paradoxically, by the time a strong partnership has developed funding may be becoming scarce as priorities shift elsewhere. (Frye and Webb, 2002, p10)

Conclusion

By the end of the pre-partnership phase, the partnership should have made significant progress including the development of:

- a shared vision and an agreed approach
- the involvement and commitment of the right organisations and the right individuals within those organisations
- good, collaborative working relations between partners based on mutual trust and respect
- an organisational structure for the partnership which is 'fit for purpose' and processes and procedures which allow business to be conducted efficiently
- a clear strategy informed by an understanding of local needs, issues and priorities.

Developing and sustaining a partnership is not easy. Box K summarises the issues faced by Local Strategic Partnerships as revealed by a survey undertaken in 2002. In addition to addressing all the issues covered by this chapter, partnerships may also have to confront and overcome the following barriers during the partnership development phase:

- *structural:* fragmentation of responsibilities across agency boundaries; non-coterminosity of organisational boundaries (see also Morris and Spicer, 2003, p19 for the impact of complexity and size of the area on the ability to establish effective Children's Fund partnerships)
- *procedural:* differences in organisational planning horizons and cycles, accountability arrangements, information systems and protocols, eg, regarding confidentiality

- *financial:* differences in budgetary cycles and accounting procedures, funding mechanisms, stocks and flows of financial resources
- *professional/cultural:* differences in ideologies and values; professional self-interest and autonomy; conflicting views about user interests and roles (see also Tomlinson, 2003, p8)
- *status and legitimacy:* organisational self-interests and autonomy
- *inter-organisational domain dissensus:* lack of agreement about organisational responsibilities (Hudson and Hardy, 2002, p54; see also Goss, 2001, pp97–99).

If the partnership has undertaken all the tasks covered in this chapter and addressed the barriers identified above, it will then be poised and ready to move into the implementation phase. This is the focus for the next chapter.

BOX K

Issues faced in developing Local Strategic Partnerships (LSPs) stakeholder engagement

Community engagement – finding a balance between inclusivity and manageable numbers; ensuring that community representation is effective; finding new ways to engage with the wider community, especially hard-to-reach groups

Partner buy-in and commitment – handling changes in memberships; partnership fatigue; maintaining interest and commitment; developing a shared sense of ownership

Accountability – interface between LSP and local democratic structures; legitimacy of the LSP as a non-elected body

Involving all as equal partners – ensuring that all partners feel that they are shaping and contributing to the partnership

Resources and capacity

Lack of resources – including lack of a budget for administration and pressure on staff resources

Funding joint action – difficulties in harmonising partners' budget-making processes, redirecting core budgets and pooling resources

Addressing partners' development needs – including strategic thinking, partners' roles and responsibilities

Developing effective ways of working

Developing a workable structure – including operation and integration of sub-groups and working groups

Streamlining existing partnerships – including ensuring effective working with other partnerships and rationalising partnerships and strategies where appropriate

Developing new working processes and systems – to prioritise and manage the workload and ensure effective communication

Performance management – including development of workable systems and reconciling different targets, systems, forms of accountability and planning frameworks

Communication – both internally among partners and with the outside world. Involves overcoming cultural differences between partners

Developing the agenda

Establishing shared priorities – including influencing partners' own agendas and agreeing priorities and actions

Establishing a role and purpose – need to demonstrate the partnership's 'added value'

External issues

Relationship with central government – including lack of joined-up thinking at the centre, difficulty of keeping up with changing national priorities and new initiatives; tension between national and community-determined priorities

Managing expectations – fear of raising public expectations that cannot be met.

Source: ODPM/Department for Transport, 2003, pp32–34

5 **Maintaining momentum**

In the last chapter we looked at the issues relevant to the development phase of partnerships ending with the preparation of a strategy. In this chapter we move to the implementation phase and consider the issues relevant to developing a detailed action or business plan; recruiting a staff team; and developing delivery and reporting mechanisms. We also consider how the commitment and motivation of the partnership can be maintained and barriers to effective partnership working overcome. The involvement of community and voluntary sector organisations, service users and children and young people in the work of the partnership is also addressed.

From strategy to action

A strategy, however comprehensive and well thought through, will not result in action without mechanisms for delivery. In some partnerships, where the primary focus is on improved co-ordination of existing services, implementation of the strategy will take place through the individual partner organisations. The role of the partnership in this case will be to monitor implementation (see section on 'Monitoring and evaluation', p68).

For other kinds of partnership, where there is a programme of work to be delivered with resources attached, delivery mechanisms will have to be put in place. The first of these is a staff team. This is likely to consist of a programme manager or co-ordinator, an administrator and a number of 'operational' staff depending on the size and nature of the programme.

There are a number of important issues to consider here in relation to partnership effectiveness. The first issue is the employing organisation. As we saw in the last chapter, the formal constitution of the partnership may determine whether or not the partnership can directly employ staff. Where this is not the case then the lead or accountable body may take on the role of employer. However, it is important that staff working for the partnership owe their loyalty and allegiance to the partnership rather than to the employing organisation; this may also be an issue where staff are seconded from a partner organisation to the partnership. Indeed, Carley and colleagues argue: 'although seconded staff can make a valuable contribution, full-time, paid staff – able to operate with a degree of independence from any one partner – are better able to promote the partnership's strategic programme and make effective use of its human and financial resources' (Carley et al, 2000). Steps need to be taken to ensure that staff fully understand the partnership's vision, purpose and objectives and how their work will contribute to their achievement. This kind of understanding can be enhanced where staff contribute to the development of a detailed action or business plan. It is important too that staff develop a relationship with the partnership board and an understanding of partners' organisations (Audit Commission, 1998a, p25).

Strategy documents typically provide too little detail to function effectively as an action plan to guide individuals' work. An important first step for the newly appointed programme manager/co-ordinator and his/her staff team will be to turn the strategy into an action plan. The purpose of the action plan is to define who is going to do what, when and how, and should be sufficiently detailed that it can operate as a 'guiding thread' for the work of the staff team. For each objective within the strategy the following need to be identified:

- delivery mechanisms – how the objective is to be met
- intended beneficiaries
- lead individual or organisation
- timescales, milestones and interim indicators of progress
- costs and sources of funding
- outputs
- outcomes
- monitoring and evaluation framework.

Production of an action plan with this level of detail is likely to take some time and go through several different drafts. Objectives can typically be met in a variety of different ways and these options will need to be appraised in the light of evidence about 'what works'. Discussions may need to take place with organisations who could potentially have a role in delivering elements of the programme; they will inevitably have their own ideas about how best to undertake certain tasks. Given these considerations it is vital that sufficient lead-in times are allowed so that the necessary appraisal and development work can take place. Timescales specified within the action plan also need to take account of factors such as the length of time it might take to recruit staff, which can also significantly affect delivery. And, finally, there needs to be consensus within the partnership around the action plan. This may be difficult to achieve. While agreement to the high-level principles and purpose contained within the strategy document may have been relatively easy to secure, the action plan will determine roles and responsibilities and the allocation of resources which may relate directly to the interests of partners and their organisations. It may be helpful to refer back to the vision and mission and to focus on the outcomes that the partnership is seeking to achieve as the basis for building consensus.

Once the action plan has been agreed work can then commence on delivering it. This may involve delivery through the staff team or through inviting bids to undertake elements of the work or through commissioning projects or other activities. Whichever method is appropriate it is important that processes and procedures are transparent and open.

Monitoring and evaluation

From the very start the partnership will be held accountable for what happens. Accountability can only occur if partners are appraised of progress, on an ongoing basis, through monitoring reports and regular reviews of activities. Constantly measuring progress towards the partnership's objectives will also facilitate the taking of remedial action where something is not working or is not working as well as it should:

> If partners do not measure their progress and compare this against their plans and available external benchmarks, such as the progress made by other similar initiatives, they may fail to identify where and how they could improve. (National Audit Office, 2001, p48)

The partnership should therefore agree early on a framework for monitoring and evaluation and set in train appropriate systems for regularly collecting and analysing information on progress towards intermediate milestones and longer-term outcomes (Health Development Agency, 2003b, p25; Thorlby and Hutchinson, 2002, p47).

There are a number of different aspects to monitoring which will be more or less relevant depending on the nature of the programme. Activities that are funded by the partnership will need to be monitored. This is typically undertaken through a requirement on the part of the partnership that it regularly completes and returns standard monitoring forms for funded projects or activites. It is important that these monitoring forms are designed in such a way that they provide the information that the partnership needs to monitor its progress and that they also fulfil any requirements for external monitoring, while at the same time not imposing too great a burden on delivery organisations.

There can be considerable resistance to monitoring within agencies, not least because multi-funded projects may have to comply with a plethora of different monitoring requirements. There may also be issues relating to the sensitivity or confidentiality of data that will also need to be addressed. Partnership staff will need to work with funded projects and organisations to make clear their requirements in relation to monitoring data and to assist organisations in the setting up of systems that both meet the partnership's requirements while at the same time addressing as far as possible delivery organisations' concerns (see Box L). Again, this can be a time-consuming task.

Individual monitoring forms from funded activities will help to build up a picture of the progress of specific projects or activities within the programme. However, the partnership is also likely to require aggregated information that allows it to review groups of activities such as all those contributing to a particular objective or, indeed, the progress of the programme as a whole. The programme manager/co-ordinator (or a designated member of staff such as a monitoring and evaluation officer) therefore needs to be able to compile regular reports on the basis of this monitoring information. Reviewing the progress of the programme should be a standing item on the agenda of the partnership:

> Programmes and services should be reviewed to ensure targets are being achieved. Partnerships need to ensure programmes and services are delivered as intended. They should assess overall programme performance, and ensure appropriate follow-up is provided. The partnership should assess the impacts on others and wider changes that result from its programmes. Where appropriate, programmes and services should be adjusted to reflect emerging needs and opportunities. (Health Development Agency, 2003b, p26)

> ## BOX L
>
> ### Monitoring and evaluation in Sure Start
>
> Sure Start programmes involve local partnerships creating an action plan with mile-stones and targets under each of Sure Start's key objectives. The programme manager is principally responsible for monitoring progress against the plan. The Sure Start Unit has also put in place an evaluation framework to assess the effectiveness of the initiative and its components.
>
> **Benefit secured**
>
> The performance framework allows partnerships to try out new approaches and test whether they work. Partnerships can assess their programme, learn from others and take action to refine their programme as a result.
>
> Source: National Audit Office, 2001

Monitoring is not the same as evaluation although the former typically contributes to the latter. Whereas monitoring is a day-to-day activity enabling the partnership to track progress and outputs, evaluation is a less frequent activity which seeks to assess the outcomes of the programme and, ultimately, its impact. Evaluation often requires additional research or investigation that allows the partnership to ask more penetrating questions than the monitoring data is able to provide answers to. Evaluation is dealt with in detail in Chapter 6. However, here it suffices to say that, as with all other aspects of partnership activity, the evaluation needs to be planned at the start of the programme, not 'added on' some time later, not least because it may have an influence on the kinds of data collected through the monitoring system and the requirements for data collection placed on funded projects and activities.

Accountability

Accountability is a major concern for those engaged in partnership working (see, for example, ODPM and Department for Transport, 2003 and Wilkinson and Craig, 2002). Most partnerships are not elected and are therefore not accountable through the electoral mechanism, yet they are frequently responsible for planning and overseeing services affecting countless people and for spending significant sums of public money. Mechanisms are therefore necessary for holding partnerships accountable for the money spent, for their progress in implementing agreed strategies and for the quality and effectiveness of the services and activities they provide. This can prove difficult, as many existing accountability mechanisms are designed for single agency activities and may not be appropriate for partnerships (Audit Commission, 1998a, p36). Indeed, in some cases, mechanisms for accountability such as inspection regimes can discourage inter-agency working. Examples of accountability arrangements are provided in Boxes M and N.

BOX M

Accountability arrangements

In Sandwell, a multi-agency partnership between the local authority and the three Primary Care Trusts (PCTs) has been commissioning all mental health services using pooled budgets since 1 April 2003. Similar arrangements have been in place for learning disability services since October 2002. Membership of the mental health partnership board comprises three elected members and one non-executive from each PCT, supported by the jointly appointed strategic partnership manager for mental health services. In addition there are a number of co-opted members drawn from Social Services, the PCTs and Sandwell Mental Health NHS and Social Care Trust, including service users and carers, who have been selected to ensure a balance of skills and experience.

Accountability is ensured by:

* approval of service strategies that meet the needs of local service users and carers and which fit with both the agreed values and principles of partner agencies and within the best value framework
* overseeing and agreeing all inter-agency planning
* performance managing the delivery of adult mental health services across Sandwell
* ensuring service user and carer views are properly represented
* producing an annual report on the action of the board to each PCT and the council.

Source: Integrated Care Network, 2003, p21

Accountability needs to operate at a number of different levels:

- accountability of the executive to the wider partnership group (where such a division exists)
- accountability of the partnership to external stakeholders including funders
- accountability of the partnership to service users and the public at large (Audit Commission, 1998a, pp36–38).

The National Audit Office, in answer to the question: what accountability and regulatory framework will best support joint working? argues that the following criteria need to be met:

> Reliable accountability depends on (i) there being clear and accurate reporting of how public money is used by each organisation and what it has achieved; and (ii) those intended to benefit from the service having adequate means of redress where quality of service is poor. (National Audit Office, 2001, p57)

They go on to emphasise that these criteria can only be achieved where the roles and responsibilities of each organisation involved in the partnership are clearly defined and understood (see also Scottish Executive, 2002, p8) and set out the following minimum requirements for sound accountability:

- clear definition of roles and responsibilities of each organisation involved and in particular partners' responsibility for ensuring propriety in the use of public money
- unambiguous targets setting out the improvement in service delivery to be achieved and over what time period
- clear statement of client groups intended to benefit
- reliable information on progress in meeting targets
- clear understanding of who is responsible for taking remedial action if progress is less than satisfactory
- audited financial statements reporting expenditure
- periodic independent evaluations to assess the achievement of planned benefits and to learn lessons.
(National Audit Office, 2001, p57)

Accountability arrangements for Sure Start

Sure Start programmes have complex accountability arrangements. 'Local partnerships agree which partner will be responsible for administering funding and producing financial accounts. The partnership as a whole is responsible for meeting Sure Start's objectives although the lead partner has the responsibility for reporting on performance to the Sure Start Unit. Each service provider operates their own complaints procedures and is responsible for the staff they employ and the services they provide. Clients can complain to their service provider in the first instance if they are not satisfied with the quality of the service they receive. The partnership has no legal responsibility for quality of service, this rests with each individual organisation within the partnership.'

Source: National Audit Office, 2001, p57

The growing number of joint working and partnership initiatives has led to concern about the increasing administrative burden that can be created, especially for smaller organisations, as a result of funding by several different government departments or agencies, each with their own separate processes for reporting on expenditure and performance and for regulation, inspection and evaluation. While there are some efforts within central government to more effectively 'join up' regulation and accountability structures and mechanisms (eg, through joint inspections and the development of the Regional Co-ordination Unit within the Cabinet Office), it is currently the case that local initiatives may still be subject to multiple inspection, accountability and scrutiny regimes.

Communication

One mechanism that will contribute to accountability is communication both between partners and between the partnership and the outside world (Frearson, 2002, p4; Health Development Agency, 2003b, p11; Civic Trust, 1999, pp107–113). Effective communication can also help defuse tensions within the partnership (NCVO/LGMB, 1993, p40):

Communication refers to the channels used by partners and stakeholders to send and receive information, keep one another informed, and convey opinions to influence the partnership's actions. (Health Development Agency, 2003b, p11)

The evaluation of Right Fit (Arc, 2002, p19) identified 'communication models that allow good access between all partners' as a factor facilitating effective partnership working. Similarly the Scottish Executive identified communication as a pre-requisite for effective inter-agency working:

It is important to continually feedback to *all* stakeholders at *all* levels in the participating organisations on progress towards meeting the objectives – communicating successes, potential barriers and action plans. Closing the communication loop is vital to success [emphasis in the original]. (Scottish Executive, 2002, pp13–14)

The partnership will therefore need to ensure that a strategy and appropriate systems are in place at the beginning of the partnership that meet the various needs for communication. These can be summarised as follows:

* communication within the partnership, ie, between partners and between staff and partners
* communication between partners and their own organisations
* communication between the partnership and the wider community.

In designing a communication strategy, attention needs to be given as to how this fits with other systems and procedures, such as those for reporting on progress (see section on 'Monitoring and evaluation' above) and for involving community and voluntary organisations and children and young people. For example, consultation events can also be used for two-way communications. Partnerships can, potentially, generate large amounts of information and a balance needs to be found between openness and swamping people with information of little use or relevance to them. The NCVO/LGMB report on partnership working with the community and voluntary sector argues that 'it is better to consider what information decision makers and others need and when, rather than to produce a regular pattern of standard report' (NCVO/LGMB, 1993, p40).

The overall objective of the partnership's communications strategy should be that the 'results of its decision making processes and activities are marketed and disseminated appropriately' (Health Development Agency, 2003b, p11). Attention will have to be given within the communications strategy to the most appropriate means for communicating with particular stakeholder groups; the timing of communications; and ways of presenting information in ways that can be readily understood and acted on by different audiences.

Maintaining and developing the partnership

Reviewing the partnership

In Chapter 3 we outlined the notion of a partnership cycle in which the form of partnership and mode of governance changes as the partnership moves from development through implementation to closure or succession. This suggests that as the partnership moves into the delivery phase a review of the partnership and its operation may be necessary and appropriate. Even if one does not subscribe to the partnership life-cycle approach, as Frearson writes: 'Maintaining a successful partnership requires a lot of energy. All partnerships large or small should be regularly reviewed to see how well they are working' (Frearson, 2002, p6; see also Health Development Agency, 2003b, p18; Audit Commission, 1998a, p28).

The review should include the partnership's terms of reference, membership, structures and processes and should identify which aspects are working well, which are working less well, and what needs to be changed or improved. The key questions that need to be asked as part of the review are shown in Box O.

BOX O

Partnership review questions

- Does the organisational structure need to be changed?
- Are partners still committed? Does commitment need to be renewed?
- Are partner organisations represented at an appropriate level of seniority?
- Are changes in the membership of the partnership required?
- Are there effective processes in place (where appropriate) for:
  - pooling or otherwise sharing budgets
  - joint commissioning
  - integrated delivery
  - data/information sharing

> - monitoring and reviewing progress
> - learning
> - shared training?
> - Is there a code of conduct for partners? Do partners abide by it? If not, is there a need for a code?
> - Have there been some 'early wins' to demonstrate benefits of partnership working?
> - Are benefits shared between partner agencies while recognising that individual partners may not all benefit to the same degree?
> - Are tensions within the partnership recognised and addressed?
> - What mechanisms are in place for the accountability of partner agencies and for the partnership as a whole?
>
> See: Civic Trust, 1999; Dean et al, 1999; Goss, 2001; Hudson and Hardy, 2002; Lowndes and Skelcher, 1998; Stoney et al, 2002; Sullivan and Skelcher, 2002)

Equally, individual partners may feel that they want to review their continued involvement in the partnership. For community and voluntary organisations especially, long-term involvement in partnerships can constitute a significant drain on limited resources and may be seen as a diversion from their primary purpose.

Wilkinson and Craig suggest the following criteria in relation to local authority members, but they could equally be applied to other organisations.

- Are representatives on the partnership the most appropriate?
- Are they fulfilling their responsibilities to the council [or parent organisation]?
- Are they receiving the most appropriate training and support?
- Is the partnership providing added value?
- What has the partnership achieved?
- Do the benefits of partnership working outweigh the costs?
  (Wilkinson and Craig, 2002, p37)

Support and capacity building

A further aspect of the review could be the support and capacity-building needs of individual partners. Partnership working can be complex and partners have varying experiences and skills in relation to working in partnership. A lack of relevant skills is most frequently mentioned in relation to small community organisations (see, for example, National Audit Office, 2001, p54). However, all partners are likely to require some training, support and capacity building in order to undertake their roles effectively.

A NCVO/LGMB publication on working in partnership with the community and voluntary sector recommends training to develop the following key skills in relation to partnership working:

- developing mutual awareness
- developing common objectives/goals
- consultation and people skills
- equal opportunities awareness and practice
- negotiation skills
- skills in creating user involvement
- managing uncertainty and change
- managing development and innovation
- monitoring and evaluation
- quality service provision (NCVO/LGMB, 1993, pp34–35).

While formal training may be an appropriate means of building capacity in relation to some issues, there are also other means available including: development meetings, away days and briefing sessions. Partnerships working in different areas on the same issues may try to foster the exchange of learning and good practice through networks, conferences, seminars and action learning sets.

Where partnerships are sponsored or promoted by central government, it is often the case that packages of advice and guidance are also available to support partnership working. In reviewing the guidance available the National Audit Office came to the following conclusion:

> We found this guidance to be of varying quality and focus – some set out general good practice principles for partnership working supported by examples, some provide specific advice relevant to particular partnership models. Most of the guidance had been prepared by departments independently of one another suggesting that there is a need for more generic guidance on the principles of joint working based on a wide range of experience. (National Audit Office, 2001, p54)

In addition to guidance and advice provided centrally this may also be available more locally. For example, the National Audit Office draws attention to the expertise within government offices in the regions and regional development agencies and quotes the example of Sure Start regional development officers who 'work from Government Offices for the Regions to advise and monitor Sure Start partnerships. The officers have their own expertise but also work to ensure that lessons learned from one partnership are disseminated more widely' (National Audit Office, 2001, p54).

Developing skills and building capacity should be aimed at enabling individual partners to make a full contribution to the partnership by building on their existing strengths and interests. Not all partners have to be equally skilled and knowledgeable in all areas of the partnership's work:

> People's knowledge and skills need to be identified, developed and applied … attention should be paid to assessing and developing individuals' knowledge and skills, and ensuring they are matched to the individual's role in the partnership. (Health Development Agency, 2003b, p17)

Maintaining enthusiasm

Maintaining the enthusiasm of partners over the long term can be difficult, especially as the partnership moves from the excitement of the development phase to the long haul of implementation. Waning enthusiasm can be a particular problem where there are delays and difficulties in relation to implementation, where operational issues such as staff recruitment come to dominate and where staff turnover results in changes in membership of the board with new members insufficiently knowledgeable of, and committed to, the partnership's purpose. However, these problems can be addressed. For example, success is a good motivator so building in some high-profile 'quick wins' to the action plan can be a useful tactic (Frearson, 2002, p4). Similarly, constantly focusing on what the partnership is seeking to achieve rather than on the operational detail can also be helpful (Audit Commission, 1998a, p26). Inclusion of progress reports on the agenda of partnership meetings (see section on 'Monitoring and evaluation' above) should help in this regard. Success needs to be publicised and celebrated and the partners should play a key role in events of this kind.

The partners themselves need to be taken care of. In particular, partnership meetings

– which may be regarded as peripheral to their 'day' jobs – should be as business-like as possible so that partners are not detained any longer than is necessary, while at the same time the atmosphere is pleasant and, perhaps, there are some opportunities for informal networking outside of meetings. Attendance might also be encouraged by different partners hosting partnership meetings. In addition, there might be a case for renewing commitment or refreshing thinking through mechanisms such as away-days or team-building exercises (Hutchinson and Campbell, 1998, p59).

Partners generally want to feel that they are contributing in the areas where they are most knowledgeable or have the most experience. Working and task groups can offer opportunities for greater involvement (see Chapter 4).

New partners, in particular, need to be supported and encouraged. At the very least they will need to be provided with a pack of information containing the strategy, action plan, recent monitoring and evaluation reports, partnership terms of reference and codes of conduct. In addition, the programme manager/co-ordinator may want to brief them prior to their first partnership meeting and the chair needs to be particularly conscious during the first few meetings where discussion assumes prior knowledge which the new member may not have.

Involving the community and voluntary sectors

Many, if not most, partnerships require or desire the involvement of the community and voluntary sectors. However, this is frequently regarded as both difficult to achieve and even more difficult to sustain. The Civic Trust, for example, identifies the following 'root causes' of difficulties in relation to community and voluntary sector involvement:

- lack of clarity over who is referred to by the term 'community' and therefore who should be involved and who are legitimate representatives
- differences of view as to what constitutes involvement and what is an appropriate level of involvement for the community and voluntary sector
- community involvement can be regarded as a time-consuming obstacle to progress
- focus on project delivery at the expense of the processes of partnership working
- expectation on the part of some partners that community involvement should be 'passive' rather than 'active'
- failure to resolve conflicts between community and voluntary groups

- relative lack of power and influence of the community and voluntary sector
- consultation, participation and capacity building are seen as administrative overheads by the partnership rather than an investment (Civic Trust, 1999, pp54–55; see also Roberts et al, 1995, p51).

In this section we discuss some of the key issues identified in the literature of relevance to the involvement of the community and voluntary sector. However, we do not pretend that this is a comprehensive guide; indeed, there are a number of such guides in existence and a selection of these is identified in the Resources section (p123).

The first question that we, and partnerships, need to consider is who we mean by the community and voluntary sector. At its broadest this can encompass:

- large national voluntary organisations such as Barnardo's, NCH, Save the Children Fund
- local voluntary organisations
- community organisations, eg, tenants' and residents' organisations, women's groups, play groups, service user and carer groups
- representatives from local communities more generally.

In determining the composition of the partnership (see Chapter 4) it is vital that there is agreement as to which of these constituencies are stakeholders and that this is kept under review. However, being a stakeholder does not necessarily mean that representation on the partnership board is appropriate. There are other ways of getting involved which may be better suited to a particular organisation or stakeholder group at any point in time.

For partnerships there are strong reasons for involving the community and voluntary sector and clear benefits of so doing (see Civic Trust, 1999, p57; Thorlby and Hutchinson, 2002, p20; Osborne, 1997; Roberts et al, 1995, p52; Pharoah et al, 1998, pp23–24). At the highest level there are arguments about democracy and the rights of communities to have a say in the decisions that affect their lives. It is also argued that community and voluntary sector involvement results in better decision-making as a result of the input of local knowledge and experience. Community involvement and participation are seen as contributing to enhanced capacity among community and voluntary organisations, leading to improved sustainability and increased ownership of local developments.

While there are clear benefits for partnerships of involving the community and voluntary sectors, the difficulties of so doing also need to be acknowledged and addressed. Firstly, voluntary groups, community groups and the community at large do not speak with one voice. Careful attention will have to be given to the mechanisms for selecting representatives to sit on the partnership in order to avoid the charge of 'token' involvement. At least some parts of the sector are typically poor in terms of resources – especially people resources – which can make long-term involvement in a partnership difficult to sustain. Individuals may lack the skills and confidence to become involved in formal partnership working. Involving the community can take time and this needs to be weighed in the balance against the need to get the partnership up and running and delivering often within tight timescales (Thorlby and Hutchinson, 2002, p20).

There are also benefits to the community and voluntary sector of getting involved in partnership working. Ourpartnership.org.uk identifies the following potential benefits:

- obtaining additional resources for your organisation
- improving your ability to identify needs and plan for the future
- increasing organisational skills and capacity
- helping build coalitions and relationships
- improving the quality of services by making them more joined up and getting new ideas
- improving the long-term sustainability of services
- may provide added appeal to funders.

BOX P

Outcomes of community involvement

Research by McArthur into regeneration partnerships in Scotland identified the following outcomes of community involvement:

- *changes to the working practices of officials* including: a more local focus, language used and style of reports: '… with a few exceptions, there is little evidence that the key agencies involved have significantly changed their practices or attitudes in the light of their experience of community partnerships'

- *shaping of regeneration strategies* including a broadening of the strategic agenda to encompass a more social dimension
- *shaping of specific policies or particular projects*
- *unforeseen consequences and spin-offs* – a community organisation established as a mechanism for involving local people and providing support to community groups has taken on a life of its own and has become a multi-faceted service provider.

Source: McArthur, 1995

Potential costs identified include the time required for administration, meetings and other partnership processes, investment necessary in research and strategy development and the need to engage in more extensive consultation processes. Ourpartnership.org.uk also warns against some possible risks, including lack of clarity about the level of commitment that may be required from the partnership; possible loss of organisational autonomy; mission drift; and the risk that some organisations may be viewed differently as a result of their involvement in a partnership arrangement:

Being part of a network or partnership imposes costs on members. This is a particular issue for the voluntary sector, where the opportunity cost of engagement in a partnership or network may be significant in terms of the day-to-day work of the agency. (Lowndes et al, 1997, p339)

The Health Development Agency recommends that: 'People, groups or organisations should be involved in the partnership if they are likely to be affected by proposed activities, or can affect the delivery and outcome of partnership objectives' (Health Development Agency, 2003b, p9).

In considering these issues the partnership may want to draw up a community involvement strategy that addresses not only who should represent the community and voluntary sector on the board but also other ways in which the sector might be involved in the work of the partnership. The Civic Trust suggests that such a strategy might address the following questions:

- Who should be involved?

- How much should they be involved?
- What will they be doing when they are being involved?
- How can this involvement be encouraged and enabled? (Civic Trust, 1999, p60; see also Thorlby and Hutchinson, 2002, p22; Health Development Agency, 2003b, p10; and Gaster et al, 1999).

A number of writers (see, for example, Civic Trust, 1999, pp58–59; Wilcox, 1994) have, following Arnstein, conceptualised participation as a 'ladder' with information-giving at the bottom and full participation in decision-making at the top. One interpretation of this approach is that full participation is the ultimate goal and other forms of involvement are, in some senses, inferior. For example, the Health Development Agency writes:

> The goal is to move towards integration of community perspectives and resources in all the processes of the partnership based on the recognition that local people usually have the clearest understanding of their own situation, and that active involvement will mean developments are more likely to be sustained. (Health Development Agency, 2003b, p10)

However, others have argued for an approach that matches forms of involvement to purpose. For example, Wilcox, while still using the 'ladder' approach to conceptualising participation, nevertheless stresses the importance of deciding the level of participation that is appropriate in the light of what the partnership is trying to achieve. He proposes five levels or stances which offer increasing degrees of control to community partners.

- *Information* – 'The least you can do is tell people what is planned.'
- *Consultation* – 'You identify the problems, offer a number of options, and listen to the feedback you get.'
- *Deciding together* – 'You encourage others to provide some additional ideas and options, and join in deciding the best way forward.'
- *Acting together* – 'Not only do different interests decide together what is best, but they form a partnership to carry it out.'
- *Supporting independent community initiatives* – 'You help others do what they want perhaps within a framework of grants, advice and support provided by the resource holder.'

Partnership operates at the levels of *deciding together and acting together* (Wilcox,

1994, p15). Wilcox concludes that: 'Participation works best when each of the key interests is satisfied with the level of participation at which they are involved' (1994, p9). He offers a set of general guidelines to assist in the process of deciding the appropriate approach to involvement (see Box Q).

BOX Q

General guidelines for thinking about community involvement

1. Ask yourself what you wish to achieve from the participation process, and what you want to help others achieve. What is the purpose?
2. Identify the different interests within a community that you wish to involve, and put yourselves in their shoes.
3. Clarify your own role, and whether you are wearing too many hats – for example, communicator of information, facilitator of ideas, controller of resources.
4. Consider what balance to strike between keeping control and gaining other people's commitment, and what levels of participation this suggests for different interests.
5. Invest as much effort in preparation as participation with outside interests.
6. Run internal participation processes to make sure your own organisation is committed and can deliver.
7. Be open and honest about what you are offering or seeking, and communicate in the language of those you are aiming to involve.
8. Make contact informally with key interests before running any formal meetings.
9. Build on existing organisations and networks – but don't use them as the only channel of communication and involvement.
10. Consider the time and resources you will need.

Source: Wilcox, 1994, p24

Thorlby and Hutchinson use the ladder approach as a means of specifying the purpose of involvement, suggesting various methods of involvement and identifying some of the issues associated with them (see Box R).

Ways of involving communities

Purpose of involvement	Approach	Issues
Informing the community	*Exhibitions and open days* Displays providing information about planned activities or opportunities.	Low cost. Turnouts may be low and unrepresentative.
	Leaflets, publications, newsletters	Can convey brief information to large numbers of people.
	Emails and website Can be useful for disseminating documents.	Not everyone has access to a computer.
	Attending meetings of 'target' groups Request a 'slot' in a group's regular meeting as a means of providing information.	May involve attending a number of meetings of different groups.
	Using other community events Having a stall at fairs, fun days or other community events can provide an opportunity to present information and talk to people.	Can reach people who would not attend a public meeting.
Seeking local views and identifying priorities	*Surveys and audits* Using survey research methods to obtain views of local people in a more structured way	Needs to be undertaken rigorously by professional researchers but local people can be involved.

Purpose of involvement	Approach	Issues
	Workshops Representatives of interest groups could attend an event to discuss issues in a structured way. Provides an opportunity to explore issues in greater depth.	Requires advance planning and organisation. May require external facilitation to get the most from it.
	Planning for real events Visual and interactive approach to planning making use of real models or plans of an area. Mainly used for exploration of new physical development possibilities.	Complex to organise; likely to require external facilitation. Can be time-consuming.
Building a common vision	*Scenario planning workshops* A structured approach to defining and discussing possible future scenarios, choosing between them and planning.	Requires careful planning; likely to require external facilitation.
	'Ideas' workshops Opportunities for wide-ranging discussion of views and development of consensus on key issues.	Allows access to a wide range of views
Conflict resolution	*Mediation/external advisers* Using external advisers or mediators can help to bring opposing sides together. *Dialogue* Regular discussion of issues with community members to prevent issues arising.	

Purpose of involvement	Approach	Issues
Long-term engagement	*Community forum* Open or membership based, provides an opportunity for discussion with a broad network of community groups and individuals of issues of concern.	Can be an inclusive method. Attendance can be large. Not always representative of local opinion. Can be difficult to manage. Role of forum in relation to partnership needs to be clarified
	Direct community elections Formal elections to elect local people to the partnership board.	Can provide legitimacy to community representatives. However, requires a very high level of commitment from candidates; need to consider how elected representatives can be held to account. Elections need to be properly organised.
	Sub-committees/consultative groups Specific groups set up as part of the partnership to undertake specific roles on which community members could play a part.	Committees and groups need to have clear roles and terms of reference.
	Community chests and projects Can provide small budgets overseen by the community to support community activities in support of main partnership work	Can help to build trust, confidence and capacity. Can also be the sources of conflict.

Source: adapted from Thorlby and Hutchinson, 2002, pp35–38

Thinking through, planning and implementing strategies for involvement of community and voluntary groups takes time which may not always be available within the tight timescales typically specified for partnership formation and development. The importance of reviewing structure and membership emphasised earlier in this chapter is therefore relevant here.

Supporting involvement

In thinking about how community and voluntary sector involvement in partnership working is supported, we need to recognise the diversity of the sector already referred to. While large and well-established national voluntary organisations may have no particular support needs, smaller local voluntary organisations and community groups are likely to require support and this will be especially the case for service users and representatives of the wider community. Failure to address support and capacity-building needs can have the effect of undermining the formally equal status of community partners due to their lack of resources or ability to exercise power and influence effectively.

For all partners there are practical issues that need to be addressed. These include:

- accessibility of meetings – including venue, time and transport
- the way in which meetings are run – language used, amount of paperwork, style of meetings
- financial support for attendance, eg, reimbursement of travel and childcare costs, payment for substitute care (see also Thorlby and Hutchinson, 2002, p33; Leiba and Weinstein, 2003, p66).

In addition, community and voluntary organisation representatives may have particular training needs (see above) that will help them operate more effectively and confidently within the partnership.

Where partners are community or sector representatives there are likely to be particular issues around their representative role including: how they will discover the views of the community or sector they represent; how they will feed back to the community or sector from the partnership; and what mechanisms should exist for the community or sector to hold the representatives accountable?

Involving children and young people

This publication is concerned with strategic partnerships for children and young people. Although many of the issues covered so far have been generic issues that relate to partnerships working in many different areas of policy, the issues of involving children and young people in partnership working is particularly germane to this account. The importance of listening to children and young people, consulting them and actively involving them in decision-making on issues affecting them has been increasingly stressed in relation to a wide range of policy initiatives including the development of the Connexions service, the Children's Fund and the Teenage Pregnancy Strategy (see also Willow, 2002; however, for a more critical perspective on youth participation, see Bessant, 2003).

As with the previous section on community and voluntary sector involvement, we do not pretend that this is a comprehensive guide to involving children and young people. A list of more detailed resources that may be helpful in this regard are included in the Resources section. In addition, McNeish and Newman (2002) summarise the lessons from an evidence review of what works in relation to children and young people's involvement; Kirby and Bryson (2003) report on extensive research and evaluation into young people's participation in public decision-making; and the National Youth Agency has produced a useful guide for the Department of Health (Department of Health, 2003b).

The Children and Young People's Unit, in its publication setting out 'core principles' for involving children and young people claims that: 'Actively involving children and young people ... will produce better services. Ultimately that will produce better outcomes for children and young people, as well as stronger communities, as departments and agencies across government draw on children and young people's contributions to shape and tailor services to meet real, rather than presumed needs' (CYPU, 2001b, p2). Further details of the benefits of children and young people's participation are provided by the CYPU on the basis of evidence and summarised in Box S.

BOX S

Benefits of involving children and young people

- *Better services:* It is accepted that the effectiveness of services depends on listening and responding to customers. Giving children and young people an active say in how policies and services are developed, provided, evaluated and improved should ensure that policies and services more genuinely meet their needs.
- *Promoting citizenship and social inclusion:* Promoting early engagement in public and community life is crucial to sustaining and building a healthy society. As successive reports from the Social Exclusion Unit have shown, listening to young people is a powerful means of persuading disadvantaged young people that they count and can contribute.
- *Personal and social education and development:* Good participation opportunities produce more confident and resilient young people. Promoting citizenship is already an important part of the government's education agenda, both pre-16 through the national curriculum and post-16. Departments and agencies that have a local presence can support participation projects that play their part in developing these skills.

Source: CYPU, 2001b, p6

As with community and voluntary sector involvement, the issues relating to involving children and young people are complex and the process can be lengthy and difficult. The CYPU has developed 'core principles' for involvement of children and young people (see Box T).

BOX T

Core principles for children and young people's participation

A visible commitment is made to involving children and young people, underpinned by appropriate resources to build a capacity to implement policies of participation.

- There is visible commitment to the principle and practice from ministers and senior management teams.
- Participation is built into the departmental or agency values and is reflected in strategic planning, resourcing, communication and business improvement activities.
- Opportunities are provided to enable relevant staff to develop the skills and attitudes to engage effectively with children and young people.

Children and young people's involvement is valued.

- Children and young people are treated honestly. That means their expectations are managed and that they are helped to understand any practical, legal or political boundaries of their involvement (see also Morris and Spicer, 2003, p30).
- The contributions of children and young people proportionate to their age and maturity are taken seriously and acted upon, and feedback from children and young people confirms this.
- Feedback on the impact of children and young people's involvement is timely and clear.

Children and young people have equal opportunity to get involved.

- Children and young people are not discriminated against or prevented from participating effectively on grounds of race, religion, culture, disability, age, ethnic origin, language or the area in which they live.
- Departments and agencies take a proactive approach in targeting those facing greatest barriers to getting involved (for example, younger children, children and young people from minority ethnic backgrounds, those living in rural areas or disadvantaged neighbourhoods, children missing school, young people in the youth justice system, refugees, traveller children, disabled and other children with special needs or special personal or family circumstances) to ensure they are aware of and take up appropriate opportunities to have their say.

- Where necessary support and opportunities for training and development are provided to children and young people so they can contribute effectively.
- Relevant information is available to children and young people in good time and in appropriate formats, is jargon free, culturally appropriate and accessible.

Policies and standards for the participation of children and young people are provided, evaluated and continuously improved.

- The rationale and success criteria against which progress will be measured are set out from the start.
- Children and young people are involved in reviewing lessons learned.
- Departments and agencies agree quality standards and codes of conduct for working with children and young people, and set out how confidentiality and child protection issues will be handled.

Source: CYPU, 2001b, pp10–11

A key element in developing a strategy for involving children and young people is agreeing a purpose for involvement and then matching forms of involvement to that purpose (see Willow, 2002, pp48–50 for an adaptation of the 'ladder' approach to children and young people's participation and also McNeish and Newman, 2002, pp190–192). The CYPU provides the following advice on setting realistic objectives and choosing appropriate methods:

> Being clear at the start about the objectives of any particular consultation or participation activity is essential. Information should be clear over how children and young people's views will be used and when decisions will be made. Honesty on all sides is needed about what is and is not likely to be influenced, and about how much decision-making can be shared with children and young people. (CYPU, 2001b, p13)

In formulating a strategy for children and young people's involvement in the work of the partnership there are a range of other issues that will also need to be addressed including the legal issues affecting children and young people's involvement; training and support needs for children and young people and other partners; and how to recognise and reward children and young people's involvement (see Connexions, 2002).

Ways of involving children and young people will be an especially important issue. While agencies may feel that there are benefits for the children and young people themselves in getting involved, these benefits may not be readily apparent to children and young people themselves, especially if they are methods that involve commitment over the long term. The range of possible methods for involving children and young people is extensive and might include:

- suggestions schemes and ways for children and young people to complain about, or comment on, services
- formal surveys and questionnaires to find out opinions
- consultation exercises using a range of possible methods including discussion groups, music or drama, games
- involving young people directly in providing services including young people producing information for other young people; designing communication tools; providing 'mentoring' advice and help; taking part in staff development and recruitment; assessing plans for new services or initiatives; evaluating services
- young people's advisory or decision-making bodies
- membership of adult-led decision-making bodies (CYPU, 2001b, p14).

The national evaluation of the Children's Fund programme identified a wide range of different processes through which the participation of children and young people was facilitated (see Box U).

BOX U

Forms of children's and young people's participation in the Children's Fund programme

Strategic development of partnerships — Participation in the strategic-level development of Children's Fund partnerships. Examples include developing, shaping or finalising delivery plans, setting themes and priorities and developing participation strategies through means such as consultation or involvement in children and young people/parents' forums.

Shaping and targeting services — Involvement in the design and targeting of services by defining levels and dimensions of need, identifying issues of access to services, service provision gaps and potential target groups and geographical areas, suggesting ways of locating and engaging target groups through means including consultation, participating in children and young people/parents' forums.

Commissioning services — Contribution to commissioning decision-making processes or in some cases the final selection/rejection of proposals and developing service level agreements either through membership of assessment panels or participating in events at which decisions are made.

Recruitment — Involvement in the recruitment of key workers such as Children's Fund staff, local evaluators, participation workers and commissioning consultants through means such as sitting on selection and interview panels.

Management and governance of partnerships and projects — Informing or feeding into the management/governance of Children's Fund partnerships through consultation, sitting on partnership management boards or through children's sub-groups of partnerships. At project/service level involvement through consultation or through project steering groups.

Spending and administering budgets	Active decision-making; spending specified budgets and grants within Children's Fund criteria.
Delivery of services and activities	Participating in delivering services and parents' involvement in delivering services and activities for children and young people.
Evaluation and research	Participating in evaluating Children's Fund services or activities at a basic level through feeding back views as users, or more involved levels of engagement such as defining outcomes and measures or being trained to be independent evaluators.
Communication, promotion and awareness	Involvement in producing promotional materials such as newsletters and developing websites.

Source: Morris and Spicer, 2003, p26

Involving children and young people using any of these methods is likely to require new and different skills and expertise from partners and partnership staff. They will need training and support to work in ways that are facilitative of children and young people's participation. Particular ways of involving children and young people will require the help of skilled and experienced youth workers and the partnership needs to budget accordingly so that these skills and experience can be bought in. This is an especially pertinent issue in relation to children and young people from more marginal groups or those with special needs. The interim evaluation of the Children's Fund identified as a particular challenge the issue of extending involvement beyond 'enthusiastic, articulate groups of children and young people who tend to be habitually involved in participative activities' (Morris and Spicer, 2003, p29). It should be remembered that a poor experience of participation is likely to deter children and young people from getting involved again.

Children and young people involved in participation work are also likely to need support. The interim evaluation of the Children's Fund identified the importance of preparing children and young people for participation through developing skills and confidence (Morris and Spicer, 2003, p27).

Evaluations of the processes of involving children and young people and the outcomes of their involvement emphasise both the difficulties of facilitating effective participation and the benefits of doing so. The Ofsted, Audit Commission and Social Services Inspectorate's report on First Wave Children's Fund partnerships concludes:

> The value of involving children in design and decision-making is widely established as the cornerstone of a preventive strategy. A key characteristic of the 28 services which are consistently good is the way in which activities are child-led. These services have developed excellent ways of involving children, enabling them to make real decisions about design and delivery. However across the whole programme, consultation with children is variable. Partnerships recognise that involving children in decision-making requires more than simply using children as representatives in adult structures. Specific projects targeted at pioneering different approaches are established, but work is at an early stage. (Ofsted et al, 2003, p41)

The Carnegie Young People Initiative (Cutler and Frost, 2001) carried out research with over 200 young people across the UK to identify the barriers to participation. Two of the main barriers identified were 'tokenism' and 'exclusiveness'. A review of young people's involvement in Connexions partnerships identifies a wide range of barriers to participation from the point of view of young people themselves and, helpfully, suggests ways in which they might be overcome (Connexions, 2002 pp20–23). Other findings from the review are summarised in Box V.

Morris and Spicer, in their interim evaluation of the Children's Fund, emphasised the time and resources that were required to develop participation work and concluded: 'incorporating children and young people's participation slowed project development down, but to good effect; participation was described as both the *most problematic* element of the work of the Partnership, as well as its *greatest achievement*' (Morris and Spicer, 2003, p27; emphasis in the original).

BOX V

Review of young people's involvement in Connexions

Participants were asked to complete a questionnaire based on their experiences of Connexions partnerships. Answers are summarised below in rank order.

Things I've learned through being involved on a Connexions committee:
- communications skills
- confidence/self-confidence
- presentation skills
- interviewing skills
- organisational skills
- committee/meeting skills
- what Connexions is and can do
- how to relate to others
- listening skills.

Things I think it would have been useful to learn/be told before I joined:
- what Connexions is and can do
- what my role will be
- how long it takes to get things done
- presentation skills.

Things I think new committee members should know:
- what Connexions is
- what commitment is required of them
- who the other stakeholders are
- how Connexions works – what we are trying to achieve
- the agenda
- presentation skills
- mutual respect.

Things I regret about being involved:
- the time commitment required – both for meetings and preparing for them – compromising school/work opportunities
- meetings can be boring
- jargon
- other young people don't get a chance to be involved – it's tokenistic
- being teased by my peers
- being patronised by my elders.

Things I enjoy about being involved:
- meeting new people and making new friends
- learning new skills
- travelling/going places/residentials
- getting my voice heard
- see changes and ideas before they happen
- being shown respect
- power
- being valued
- receiving incentives/rewards
- feeling professional
- making a positive impact on young people's lives/helping mould a new youth-orientated organisation.

Things I've found hard or frustrating about being involved:
- jargon
- patronising attitudes with a tokenistic attitude
- level and amount of preparation required for meetings
- timing of meetings
- level of commitment required – not always being shown by all on the committee
- the length of time it takes to get anything done – red tape
- travel/transport,

Things I would still like to know to be a better decision-maker:
- all the facts – without the jargon
- an understanding of the jargon
- wider knowledge of the situation both locally and nationally
- the other committee members
- what service-level agreements are
- more experience.

Things I think the other committee members should know or do to make things easier for everyone:
- respect other people's opinions
- be approachable – work with others, not against them
- don't use jargon
- don't be too formal.

Source: Connexions, 2002 pp18–20

For partnership working to be effective requires individuals from different organisations to work together towards an agreed common goal. This can be a complex and difficult process especially where there is no prior history of partnership working in the locality that can be built upon (see, for example, Morris and Spicer, 2003, p18). The most effective partnerships are those that are able to overcome the barriers to partnership working that they will inevitably encounter.

Conclusion

This chapter has reviewed the evidence on the factors that contribute to keeping partnerships going as they move into the implementation phase and acknowledged that different skills, structures and personnel may need to be involved. However, the informal aspects of partnership working – how people feel about the partnership and its achievements and each other – are also crucially important to maintaining enthusiasm and commitment to the partnership and its purpose.

This chapter has also briefly discussed some of the issues relating to involvement of the community and voluntary sectors and children and young people. These are both complex and difficult areas which require more extensive consideration than it has been possible to give them here. Nevertheless, getting these aspects right can contribute significantly to the success of the partnership and bring positive benefits to all those involved.

Some strategic partnerships for children and young people are responsible for time-limited programmes and so will have a natural end-point. In other cases partnerships are set up as semi-permanent structures with an indefinite life-span. Time-limited partnerships will want, towards the end of their life, to review their achievements and consider what the learning points are for their own and other organisations. They will also want to consider whether or not some of their activities or services have been particularly effective and should, therefore be 'mainstreamed'. Partnerships with a longer life-span will also want to consider, at regular intervals, what impact they are having and whether or not they need to change direction. In the next chapter we focus on the outcomes from partnership working and how they are measured.

6 Measuring progress: evaluating strategic partnerships

As the previous two chapters have demonstrated, partnership working can be resource-intensive and difficult to do effectively. There is, therefore, a need to provide evidence that partnership working is effective in order to justify the additional costs incurred. This requires systems for measuring and evaluating progress and impact. Evaluation also serves a further function; it provides information to the partners concerning which aspects of the partnership's work are going well and which require review or reconsideration thus contributing to the ongoing process of organisational learning (see also Thorlby and Hutchinson, 2002, p54). As the Health Development Agency notes:

> Strategy needs to be intelligent. It should be informed by feedback from monitoring key performance indicators (process, outputs and outcomes). By building the capacity to gather information about performance and feedback from local communities/other stakeholders across the partnership, strategy development and implementation become dynamic processes which continually adapt to a changing environment. (Health Development Agency, 2003c, p32)

Evaluating partnership processes, activities and outcomes can be difficult. Research into cross-cutting issues affecting local government examined approaches to evaluation and concluded:

> Evaluation of the efficacy of implementation processes and the impact of policies is fundamental to learning about 'what works', to inform future policy and influence organisational response. The overall impression is that feedback mechanisms that would enable learning are weak. Evaluation of cross-cutting issues is inherently difficult, and there is a tension between the timescales needed to show results and the speed of politically-driven policy change. There is a need for a longer term focus on the achievement of outcomes, and new approaches to dealing with issues such as externalities and synergy. The lack of agreed criteria for or evidence of success in relation to cross-cutting issues compounds the under-analysis of the problems, and means that to a very considerable extent policy development is proceeding 'blind'. (DETR, 1999, pp44–45)

This research finding raises a number of key issues of relevance to evaluation that will be covered in this chapter. Firstly we examine what the literature tells us about developing a partnership evaluation strategy. We then review a number of different approaches to evaluation and evaluation frameworks and consider their implications for the scope of partnership evaluation and the kinds of questions evaluation seeks to answer. Finally, we discuss some of the barriers to partnership evaluation and consider the pre-requisites for successful evaluation.

The focus of this chapter is evaluation undertaken by or on behalf of the partnership. However, it should be remembered that the partnership is likely to be subject to other external audits, reviews and inspections which can also contribute to the ongoing process of measuring and reviewing progress. For example, many partnerships will be subject to regular reviews of their performance carried out by the sponsoring government department or the government office for the regions on behalf of the sponsoring government department. These reviews are often conducted on the basis of comprehensive and challenging performance management frameworks which contain extensive criteria against which performance is judged and which can also provide the basis for partnerships' own self-assessment.

Partnerships for children and young people and the services they provide are also likely to be subject to inspection from the Social Services Inspectorate, Ofsted and the Audit Commission. However, these agencies increasingly recognise that multiple inspections of the same services by different inspectors working to different inspection frameworks are not helpful. As a result there is a move towards joint inspection processes and this is identified as a priority in the Children Act 2004 (see Chapter 1). Box W shows the joint Children's Fund inspection criteria relating to the question: 'Is the use of the Fund well-managed?'

Finally, most partnership initiatives that are part of large national programmes will be subject to national programme evaluations. Any local evaluation activity should be consistent with, and not duplicate, what is going on nationally. However, national evaluations do not always provide feedback or information on individual local partnerships at a level of detail that would allow them to review their activities. Nevertheless, national evaluation reports can provide useful benchmarks against which local partnerships can measure their own progress.

BOX W

Children's Fund inspection criteria relating to the question: 'Is the use of the Fund well-managed?'

- Is the partnership working well and is the membership appropriate?
- Are children appropriately involved in decision-making and management?
- Are suitable checks being made for health, safety, child protection and the probity of finance?
- Does the partnership have access to suitable management and administrative support?
- Is there effective communication with key stakeholders including carers and schools?
- Is the partnership receiving suitable strategic management and practical support from lead and partner statutory agencies?
- Are there effective systems for monitoring and evaluation that are supported by the collection and analysis of effective management information, and is appropriate action taken as a result?
- Are the lessons which are being learned being integrated into existing policy and provision and is good practice being identified and disseminated?

Source: Ofsted et al, 2003

Developing an evaluation strategy

In the previous chapter the importance of putting in place effective systems for monitoring progress was stressed. Monitoring is not, however, the same as evaluation although routinely collected monitoring data is likely to feed into evaluation. Monitoring refers to the day-to-day recording of activities and outputs and, taken as a whole, monitoring data should constitute a descriptive record of the partnership's work. Monitoring data typically enables us to answer the question: what did we do? Evaluation, by contrast, takes a longer-term view and asks questions about effectiveness, cost-effectiveness and impact. It typically requires the collection of additional data beyond what is available through routine monitoring information.

As with so many other aspects of partnership working, evaluation needs to be planned and systems put in place at an early stage. The partnership will therefore need to develop an evaluation strategy and action plan that addresses the following questions:

1. Are the partners committed to and supportive of evaluation? Do they share a common understanding of its purpose?
2. What should be evaluated? The partnership and partnership processes? Implementation of the partnership's strategy? The impact of the partnership?
3. What kinds of questions should the evaluation provide answers to?
4. Are there particular principles or a particular approach that the partners wish to see reflected in the evaluation?
5. Are there other evaluation activities going on? How will this evaluation fit with others and avoid duplication?
6. What resources – financial and human – are available to undertake the evaluation?
7. Over what timescale should the evaluation take place? Are there key reporting dates that fit with the partnership's planning cycle?
8. Who has overall responsibility for ensuring that the evaluation takes place?

While the responsibility for ensuring that evaluation takes place within agreed timescales is likely to rest with the programme manager on behalf of the partnership, this does not resolve the issue of who should actually undertake the evaluation work. Much of the information that is necessary for evaluation will be held by the partnership. However additional material may have to be collected and all the relevant information has to be collated and interpreted. Who should undertake this task? The choice is essentially between self-evaluation and independent evaluation by someone external to the partnership. There are advantages and disadvantages to both approaches. Self-evaluation can result in greater ownership of the results of the evaluation leading to a greater willingness to learn lessons. However, it is not always the case that there is someone within the partnership who has the appropriate skills to undertake evaluation work. Also it may be difficult for an internal evaluator to be sufficiently detached to adopt an appropriately critical stance.

Appointing an independent consultant to undertake the evaluation can be costly and, without a clear specification and appropriate management of the process, may not result in information that is of use to the partnership. For evaluation by an independent consultant to be successful it is important that the partnership is clear about the scope of the evaluation – what they want to know – and that this is set out in a written specification. A good specification might be expected to contain the following information:

- the objectives or purpose of the evaluation
- background information on the partnership and programme to be evaluated
- scope of the evaluation – which areas or activities are to be evaluated and the issues to be covered
- timescale within which the evaluation should be completed
- the approach and/or methods to be used
- budget available for the work
- outputs from the evaluation – format within which findings should be presented including any interim reports or presentations
- the process for submitting proposals including deadlines for submission, format for proposals and criteria for selection. (Thorlby and Hutchinson, 2002, p58)

The partnership may be obliged by the rules governing procurement within the accountable body to invite competitive bids for externally commissioned work. Even where there is no such obligation it is generally worth seeking a few proposals so that different approaches can be compared. It may also be helpful to seek advice from others in the local area about possible consultants who might be able to undertake evaluation work.

Approaches to evaluation
A key aspect of planning evaluation that the partnership will have to consider is the kind of evaluation that it wants and the approach to be adopted. In a recent paper Lewis and Utting argue that while 'a welcome emphasis has been placed on providing holistic, developmentally appropriate services for children through multi-agency partnerships ... this adds further complication to the task of establishing "what worked"' (Lewis and Utting, 2001, p1). One of the difficulties is the lack of clarity over what or who the evaluation is for. Lewis and Utting (2001, p2) distinguish between evaluation for accountability, evaluation for development and evaluation for knowledge, and then argue that evaluation methods and approach need to appropriately reflect that purpose.

While existing frameworks may be inadequate for the task, there are nonetheless a number of different approaches to evaluating partnerships that have been developed (see Sullivan and Skelcher, 2002, chapter 10 for a comprehensive account).

During the 1980s and 1990s much of the evaluation work in relation to partnership activity, particularly in the area of regeneration (eg, City Challenge and Single Regeneration Budget) was undertaken within a 'value-for-money' framework. The main focus of value-for-money evaluations was the questions of economy and efficiency and, to a lesser extent, effectiveness. Analysis of inputs and their relationship to outputs led to conclusions being drawn about the costs and benefits of particular interventions (Sullivan and Skelcher, 2002, pp188–190). However, value-for-money evaluations had significant drawbacks. Firstly, they typically took place at the end of a programme and therefore did not facilitate learning and change during the lifetime of the programme. Secondly, they allowed very little to be said about what difference the programme made to its beneficiaries or the wider community. Thirdly, they imposed a heavy administrative burden on programmes in terms of detailed recording of outputs. In assessing the benefits created by partnerships, attention should also be given to the costs incurred in creating those benefits.

Furthermore, an assessment of costs should include both direct costs and also indirect, or 'opportunity' costs. The main opportunity cost is the time partners spend in partnership meetings or in other activities relating to the partnership. However, few partnerships make full estimates of these costs and so are unable to reliably demonstrate value for money (Audit Commission, 1998a, p36). In addition, the costs of *not* working in partnership should also be taken into account. In the case of partnership working for children and young people this can go beyond the distress and inconvenience to service users of poorly co-ordinated services and include increased risk of harm and abuse.

More recently there has been a shift towards evaluations that focus on outcomes rather than outputs and look at a wider set of issues than value for money. However, outcome-focused evaluations can be technically difficult to undertake. It is not always easy to identify causal relationships between specific interventions and outcomes. For example, indicators may show an improvement in child health in a particular area. However, there are a wide range of different factors that contribute to child health and it is often difficult to determine which intervention (if any) led to the improvement. A related problem is the difficulty of 'establishing the counter-factual' or, estimating what might have happened without the partnership (Pollitt, 2003, p46).

A further difficulty relates to timescales. For partnerships whose objectives relate, in broad terms, to improving the health, well-being and life-chances of children and young people, outcomes are only likely to be apparent in the long term. However, partnerships typically have to demonstrate that they are making a difference in the short to medium terms. It is therefore necessary to identify milestones on the way to the achievement of outcomes that can be measured in the short term. However, this is not always easy. Furthermore, many of the outcomes typically sought by partnerships are relatively difficult to quantify and measure, for example, improved relations between agencies or enhanced community capacity.

The difficulties associated with establishing objective and quantifiable measures of programme effects, together with a recognition of the importance of process, led to the development of what came to be known as process-outcome evaluation, epitomised by the work of Guba and Lincoln (1981).

The 'balanced score card' framework for evaluation is one example of the application of a process-outcome approach. Originally developed for use in the private sector, it has also been applied in relation to public sector programmes. For example, the Accounts Commission (Scotland) offers guidance to community safety partnerships on performance measurement using this approach (Accounts Commission, 2000) but it could equally be applied to children's and young people's partnerships. The balanced score card is based on four different perspectives of organisational effectiveness; appropriate performance indicators are developed in relation to each of the four perspectives. These indicators are unique to the partnership and relate to its strategic priorities and objectives. Indicators can be either quantitative and/or qualitative. The aim is for the partnership to build a balanced and comprehensive picture of their performance; the perspectives cover both the outcomes the partnership is seeking to achieve and how effectively it is working to achieve them (see Figure 2).

The increasing emphasis given to the way in which process affects outcomes has influenced the development of what have come to be known as 'theory-based' approaches to evaluation which require that the links between process and outcomes are made explicit. On example is the 'theory of change' approach. Originally developed in the United States to evaluate 'comprehensive community based initiatives', the theory of change approach has been defined as 'a systematic and cumulative study of the links between activities, outcomes and contexts of the initiative' (Connell and

Figure 2 **Balanced Score Card Approach**

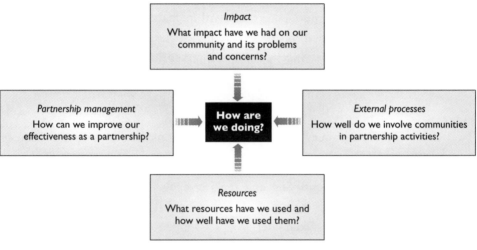

Source: adapted from Accounts Commission, 2000

Kubisch, 1998, p16). The key aspect of this approach is the importance attached to understanding the overall vision (or theory) of a programme. This includes the long-term outcomes and the particular strategies that are intended to produce change. Theory generation is undertaken by those with responsibility for planning and implementing the programme. As part of the evaluation they are asked to discuss how the programme can best produce positive outcomes and to make explicit the connections between interventions and outcomes. It is suggested that this approach has the following benefits.

- A theory of change can sharpen the planning and implementation of a programme.
- The evaluation will have a clearer idea of what to measure – final and intermediate outcomes and processes – and when and how to measure those elements.
- A theory of change specifies how interventions will lead to outcomes and the contextual conditions that may affect them. As such it suggests likely relationships between cause and effect that can go some way towards addressing problems of attribution of impact (Sullivan and Skelcher, 2002, pp192–193).

A complementary 'theory-based' approach is realistic evaluation, which was developed to address the difficulties posed by complex social programmes for measurement of effects and assigning causality. Pawson and Tilley (1997) argue that evaluation of social programmes takes place within changing contexts which can be as influential as the intervention itself in terms of the outcomes that result. The relationship between context, mechanism (or intervention) and outcomes is encapsulated within the formula:

$$C \text{ (Context)} + M \text{ (Mechanism)} = O \text{ (Outcome)}$$

This leads to a focus within evaluation on three questions: why does a programme or intervention work? For whom does it work? And in what contexts does it work?

Finally, a concern with identifying and making explicit the different values that underpin evaluation has led to stakeholder or pluralist approaches to evaluation. These argue that different stakeholder groups – funders, beneficiaries, partners and providers – are all likely to have different perspectives on a programme or initiative. Evaluation therefore needs to examine programme effectiveness from all these different perspectives.

In practice, contemporary evaluations of partnerships and partnership programmes combine elements from all of these different approaches. For example, Thorlby and Hutchinson (2002, p56) propose the following very simple framework for evaluating partnerships using four key dimensions, in which it is possible to discern elements of value-for-money and outcome-focused evaluation approaches:

1. *Rationale:* Do the partnership's vision and aims match the needs identified? Is the programme appropriately targeted? Are conditions changing and if so is there a need for the programme to change?
2. *Effectiveness:* What outputs have been delivered? How do they compare with the partnership's aims and objectives? How effective has the partnership been?
3. *Cost-effectiveness:* Compares inputs with outputs. What are the unit costs? Does this represent value for money?
4. *Impact and significance:* Who is benefiting and how? What is the nature and extent of the impact and how does this compare with local conditions? What difference has the programme made?

The Health Development Agency has produced a guide to assessing partnership working, *The working partnership* (2003a, b and c). It was initially designed in response to the World Health Organisation's Investment for Health initiatives and was launched in Verona in 1998 and came to be known as 'The Verona Bench-mark'. It is intended to help a wide variety of different kinds of partnerships assess their progress against evidence-based criteria. This framework combines elements of theory-based and stakeholder approaches.

Hudson and Hardy (2002) have developed a tool for assessing partnerships based on extensive research, principally in the areas of health and social care, and resulting in the development of success criteria for partnerships which focus very much on partnership processes. These have been distilled into six partnership 'principles' which form the basis of an evaluation framework. These six principles are:

1. Acknowledgement of the need for partnership
2. Clarity and realism of purpose
3. Commitment and ownership
4. Development and maintenance of trust
5. Establishment of clear and robust partnership arrangements
6. Monitoring, review and organisational learning (Hudson and Hardy, 2002, pp53–61).

Scope and evaluation questions

Whichever broad approach to evaluation is adopted, decisions will need to be made about the scope of the evaluation and the kinds of questions that might be asked. These might cover any or all of three aspects of the partnership and its activities.

- Partnership processes – how the partnership operates on a day-to-day basis.
- Partnership performance – what is the difference made to the way in which things are done?
- The outcomes of the programme or set of activities that the partnership is responsible for.

The issues and evaluation questions associated with each of these will be considered in turn.

Partnership processes

This area covers the way in which the partnership conducts itself and runs its activities including meetings, decision-making, membership, participation, communications, leadership, management, financial control, systems and procedures.

Roaf (2002) identifies the following characteristics of good inter-agency practice which could provide a bench-mark against which to measure partnership processes:

- formal commitment and support from senior management and from political to practitioner level
- formal and regular inter-agency meetings to discuss ethical issues, changes in legislation and practice, gaps in provision and information-sharing at all levels to develop short and long-term strategies
- common work practices in relation to legislation, referral/assessment, joint vocabulary, agreed definitions, procedures and outcomes
- common agreement of the client groups and collective ownership of their problems, leading to early intervention
- mechanisms for the exchange of confidential information
- a framework for collecting data and statistical information across all agencies that can inform all practice including ethnic monitoring
- monitoring and evaluation of services in relation to inter-agency work
- joint training in order to understand each other's professional roles. (Roaf, 2002, p87)

Partnership performance

The key question here is: what is the nature and extent of the benefits of partnership working? Here what we are looking for are changes in the way partners and their organisations behave. Thorlby and Hutchinson list the following possible benefits that might accrue:

- consensus
- innovation
- efficiency
- stronger voice
- joined-up services
- quality
- scale and coverage

- bending mainstream programmes.
  (Thorlby and Hutchinson, 2002, p60)

Pettit (2003, para 5.2) suggests, in addition, increased trust between partners; enhanced capacity in the community and voluntary sector; and increased awareness and learning between staff from different agencies.

Stewart and colleagues identify three inter-related indicators of partnership success as follows:

1. Their ability to 'endure, evolve and become stronger over time'. This will involve:
    - breaking down demarcation lines
    - greater mutual understanding
    - raised profile of the partnership's work within partner organisations
    - pooled resources
    - expanded fields of responsibility as the partnership develops.

2. 'Substantive achievements' which, it is acknowledged, may be difficult to demonstrate but might include:
    - the development of projects or further partnerships which are then 'spun off' and become self-sustaining
    - organising better access to external funding sources
    - facilitating collaboration between partners on areas of work unrelated to the core partnership agenda.

3. 'Process-related and symbolic achievements' including:
    - a shared consciousness or increased awareness of issues
    - organisational learning and a broadening of professional horizons
    - breaking down of parochial attitudes.
      (Stewart et al, 1998, p49)

For Pollitt a key, overarching evaluation question would be: has partnership working 'produced *integrated* policies, or are there still contradictions, duplications and fragmentations in policy delivery' (Pollitt, 2003, p45). Roberts and colleagues identify four dimensions around which evaluation of partnership processes could take place (see Box X).

BOX X

Characteristics of effective partnerships

Visibility – partners' relations with one another

Key questions:

- Is there a clear vision jointly developed and accepted?
- Has the vision been translated into strategic objectives?
- Is there consensus on the programmes for achieving the objectives and the mechanisms for delivering them?
- Does the partnership hold inductions or 'teach-ins' for new members or employees in relation to their mainstream and partnership activities?
- Is there clarity about:
  - What benefit each partner hopes to achieve?
  - What each partner is bringing?
  - What each expects from others?
- Is there openness and transparency to people outside the partnership?
  - Does it have easy points of entry for prospective partners?
  - Are there formal mechanisms for introducing the views and expertise of other agencies into partners' decision-making processes, eg, advisory groups.

Resource-sharing

Key questions:

- To what extent do partners share information?
- Are there valuable local resources outside existing partnership arrangements? If so, what steps have been taken to draw them in?

Institutionalising partnership

Key questions:

- Is there a standard practice of consulting partner agencies about statements of/changes in policy?

- When major plans/strategies are being prepared, are these undertaken jointly or individually?
- Have there been changes to internal working arrangements to facilitate inter-disciplinary co-operation?
- Are there inter-agency working groups relating to specific policy areas?

Changing partners' behaviour

Key questions:

- How far does inter-agency teamwork permeate each partner organisation? Is communication confined to senior members/officers or does it run throughout their respective organisations?
- Are there periodic secondments or volunteer placements between agencies to facilitate the cross-fertilisation of expertise and philosophies?

Source: Roberts et al, 1995, pp91–94

Harrison and colleagues identify the following characteristics of successful partnerships but acknowledge that they are an ideal to aim for rather than a norm that can be expected:

- involve more than two agencies or groups possibly from more than one sector and include the key stakeholders, ie, those affected by the problem or with a responsibility for developing solutions
- have common aims, acknowledge the existence of a common problem and have a shared vision of what the outcome should be
- have an agreed plan of action or strategy to address the problem
- acknowledge and respect the contribution that each of the agencies can bring to the partnership
- are flexible in that they seek to accommodate the different values and cultures of participating organisations
- consult with other relevant parties that are not part of the partnership
- exchange information and have agreed communication systems
- have agreed decision-making structures
- share resources and skills

- involved the taking of risks
- establish agreed roles and responsibilities
- establish systems of communication between partners and other relevant agencies.
  (Harrison et al, 2003, p4)

Atkinson and colleagues distinguish between benefits to agencies, such as offering them a broader perspective, a better understanding of the issues and improved inter-actions with other agencies, and benefits to individual professionals such as reward-ing work with professionals from other backgrounds and making one's own job easier by reducing the time spent solving problems (Atkinson et al, 2002, p93).

In considering the benefits of partnership working one also needs to weigh in the balance the additional costs imposed by working in partnership. Pettit identifies the following:

- time investment
- increased management difficulties
- difficulties of information-sharing
- maintaining professional identities; feeling de-skilled and/or becoming absorbed into another agency's organisational culture.
  (Pettit, 2003: para 6.7)

Partnership outcomes

Evaluating the outcomes from partnership working is 'often hard to do at all, and very hard to do well' (Pollitt, 2003, p46). As Leiba and Weinstein write: 'There is plenty of evidence that breakdowns of communication between professionals or between service users and professionals can harm users. It is more difficult to show that user involvement and multi-professional working benefits users and carers ...' (2003, p76). Similarly, Pollitt argues that meeting the strict requirements for a full evaluation of 'joined-upness' would be hard to satisfy (2003, p45).

The precise outcomes to be measured in relation to any particular partnership will depend on the objectives, the range of interventions and the timescales over which they will be achieved. However, there are a number of generic evaluation questions that can be used to inform the development of more specific evaluation questions. These can be summarised as follows.

- What has the partnership achieved that could not or would not have been achieved without the partnership?
- Is the target group being reached? Are benefits equitably distributed?
- Have there been any unintended or unforeseen impacts?

There have been a number of major evaluations of partnerships and, as Goss writes, their broad conclusions are consistent with each other. These are that participants see partnership working as generally positive although hard to do in practice as a result of significant obstacles which can take a long time to overcome. She concludes:

> The consensus among researchers is that partnership arrangements consume a huge amount of time, energy and resources to create relatively limited outcomes and outputs … While the potential is considerable, results have so far been small-scale. While partnerships and networks seem to be good at strategy, planning, document writing, research, data-gathering and so on, delivery is harder. (Goss, 2001, p95)

This emphasis on the *potential* of partnerships to achieve positive outcomes rather than the actuality of positive outcomes is typical of a number of research and evaluation studies. For example, Gardner concludes that joint working has the potential to provide positive outcomes for children and families including a more integrated, timely and coherent response to complex human problems; fewer unnecessary contacts and processes for service users to cope with; more efficient transfer of information; cost-efficiency; and some reduction of unnecessary risk (Gardner, 2003, p141). However, more positive outcomes from partnership working have been reported (see Box Y for one example).

BOX Y

Listening to Young People: outcomes from partnership working

The Cornwall and Isles of Scilly Health Promotion Service and Cornwall Youth Service have been working in partnership to facilitate the planning and promotion of high quality attractive and relevant health services for young people. The 'Listening to Young People' project aimed to reduce the levels of teenage pregnancy in the project area by making existing primary care services more accessible to the 13–19-year-old age group.

Research undertaken by the project has demonstrated the following outcomes:

- the fostering of a sense of team and the empowerment of those traditionally at the bottom of the hierarchy in the primary healthcare setting (ie, reception staff) who play a key role in being the front line of communications
- an interactive learning structure which creates a framework where there is an opportunity to negotiate change
- an opportunity for primary healthcare teams to examine the service they offer young people and, because the whole team is involved, to obtain a clear idea of the whole service from the first point of contact
- the fears, perceptions and barriers to existing sexual health services identified by young people at the beginning of the project have been shown to be justified and real through the subsequent work with primary healthcare teams
- every practice recognised the need for some changes to be made.

Source: Hughes, 2003

Barriers to effective evaluation

Dean and colleagues, as part of their research into partnership working in Scotland, asked stakeholders what they thought were the difficulties associated with establishing monitoring and evaluation frameworks. The following issues were identified:

- determining appropriate success indicators
- determining appropriate levels of success, ie, quantifying what constitutes 'poor' or 'good' performance
- whether success should be measured against local or national standards
- the absence of reliable information sources leading to the abandonment of desired indicators; sometimes indicators are chosen because they are straightforward to measure
- the potential for inconsistency or conflict between measures
- the need to determine a wide range of indicators but to distinguish between

those which might be regarded as 'headline' for inclusion in regular board reports
- the development of common information systems and databases (Dean et al, 1999, p27).

Similarly DETR (2000b, para. 5.1) identified the following barriers to successful partnership evaluation.

- Collaborative working is typically instigated to address strategic/locality-wide issues and it is often difficult to select measures of success attributable to the partnership alone.
- Partnerships in the early stages of development are unlikely to have agreed terms of reference beyond broad aims and therefore it is difficult at this stage to identify criteria against which success can be measured.
- Successful evaluation is dependent upon the importance placed on it by individuals involved in the partnership.
- The level of co-ordination and the investment in time and resources required to effectively evaluate can be considerable.
- It is difficult to define appropriate, quantifiable measures of success.

Pre-requisites for effective evaluation
For partnership evaluation to be effective a number of pre-requisites need to be met. Firstly, the purpose of the evaluation needs to be understood and agreed by all stakeholders. Secondly, evaluation depends on there being a comprehensive strategy and action plan that clearly specifies objectives, relates these to outputs, outcomes and timescales and assigns clear responsibility for their progression. Thirdly, what counts as a successful outcome needs to be discussed and agreed by the partners and related to baseline information. And, finally, there needs to be a robust monitoring system in place together with effective mechanisms for measuring outputs and outcomes (DETR, 2000b, para 5.1; Health Development Agency, 2003c, p32; Audit Commission, 1998a, p310; National Audit Office, 2001, p48).

Measuring partnership progress should not be an 'add-on' or after-thought; it needs to be built into planning from the start and the outcomes from review and evaluation should result in reflection, learning and change in order to make partnership activities more effective (Health Development Agency, 2003a, p55). For example, the

National Audit Office's review of early years development and childcare partnerships identified what has worked well, risks to success and key lessons (see Box Z).

BOX Z

Early Years Development and Childcare Partnerships

What has worked well
- leaders regard the work as important
- building relationships around shared goals
- resources to underpin partnership working
- leadership skills
- working arrangements support partnership working
- sharing information in practices that work.

Risks to success
- key parties not engaging in the partnership
- funding arrangements place disproportionate burden on partners
- impact of short timescale.

Key lessons
- partnerships need support from local councillors and senior council officials to ensure that partners give sufficient priority to the work of the partnership and resources are not diverted elsewhere
- good leadership is needed to create effective working relationships between partners
- partnerships need to focus on their aims and on establishing and carrying out the tasks needed to achieve those aims.

Source: National Audit Office, 2001, p76

Conclusions

In measuring the progress of partnerships for children and young people we are centrally concerned with the following questions: Is the partnership achieving positive outcomes for children and young people that could not be achieved by an agency or agencies acting alone? Precisely what those outcomes are would have to be elaborated in the light of the specific objectives set for or by the partnership itself. However, it is, perhaps, worth re-stating the five headline outcomes set by the government in relation to children and young people:

- being healthy: enjoying good physical and mental health and living a healthy lifestyle
- staying safe: being protected from harm and neglect and growing up able to look after themselves
- enjoying and achieving: getting the most out of life and developing broad skills for adulthood
- making a positive contribution: to the community and to society and not engaging in anti-social or offending behaviour
- economic well-being: overcoming socio-economic disadvantages to achieve their full potential in life.
  (HM Treasury 2003, p14)

Further questions then relate to how the outcomes from partnership working are being achieved, which might cover both what the partnership is doing (strategies, interventions and services) and how they are going about it (processes). These questions might include: what is the partnership doing to achieve positive outcomes for children and young people? and: how effectively is the partnership conducting its business?

Understanding partnership effectiveness may also require an examination of the context in which it is working and, more specifically, the contextual features that help or hinder partnership effectiveness.

If we are to justify the additional costs imposed by partnership working then we will need to develop robust approaches and systems for evaluating partnerships, their process and the outcomes of their work. However, at the same time, we need to be mindful that *measurement* of their activities is not the central issue rather it is the activities themselves. So as Perri 6 and colleagues caution we need to ensure that overly rigid systems for performance measurement do not become a 'strait jacket' that effectively kills off integration. Rather it is better to encourage 'continual strategic conversations' about outcome measures, targets, and systems of monitoring and accountability (Perri 6 et al, 1999, pp44–45).

7 Conclusion

Issues relating to children and young people are currently high on the political agenda together with a growing recognition in politics, policy and practice that services for children and young people need to be planned and delivered in new ways that cross traditional service and professional boundaries. The government's agenda includes the development of both strategic and operational partnerships as a primary means of developing more effective and, crucially, more joined-up services for children, young people and their families. Effectiveness is seen in terms of delivering improved outcomes.

Partnership working is widely applauded in principle but can be difficult to put into practice successfully. It requires careful planning, commitment and enthusiasm on the part of partners, the overcoming of organisational, cultural and structural barriers and the development of new skills and ways of working. To assist localities develop the strategic partnerships that are becoming an increasingly prominent feature on the local landscape, there is now a wealth of experience and expertise on which to draw. As this book shows, much, but by no means all, of this experience and expertise derives from policy areas other than those relating to children and young people, for example, regeneration, community safety and health. Furthermore, as partnership working has become established so it has become the focus for research and evaluation, which has generated a significant body of evidence about 'what works', including a number of guides and toolkits, on which this book draws.

Across the literature relating to partnership working that has been surveyed in the course of writing this book, it is striking that, whatever the underlying approach to, or theories about, partnership working, there is a wide-ranging consensus about 'what works' in relation to establishing and developing partnerships. Key issues include the importance of planning, the need to relate organisational form, governance structure and processes to strategic purpose, the importance of involving the right people from the right organisations in the right ways, the need to develop a shared vision and to relate this to an appropriately resourced strategy and action plan. Finally, the literature emphasises the fact that partnerships are not just structures but consist of individuals from a variety of different organisational cultures and professional backgrounds who need to learn to work together in, perhaps, new ways.

Similarly, the literature on maintaining and sustaining partnerships has a number of strong themes running through it including the importance of leadership, the need to support partners and develop their skills and capacities, the role of monitoring and evaluation in ensuring that partners retain a focus on outcomes and the need to keep partnership structures, terms of reference and membership under review to ensure that they continue to be effective in relation to strategic objectives.

All of these issues are common to almost all partnerships, no matter what the area of policy is with which they are grappling. And, again, the literature is remarkable in its consistency no matter what the specific policy areas covered. Strategic partnerships for children and young people do, however, differ in one important respect. While almost all partnerships have to address the challenging issue of how best to involve the community and voluntary sectors, the broader community and service users, partnerships for children and young people face the additional question of how best to involve children and young people. The literature on involving the community and voluntary sectors is extensive and, again, while offering a range of different approaches to involvement is, nonetheless, fairly consistent in terms of 'what works' within these different approaches. The literature on involving children and young people in partnership working is less extensive but there is, instead, an increasing body of literature on involving children and young people more generally that can, and should, be applied to partnership working.

Given the extent, range and consistency of the evidence on partnership processes, it is possible to offer practical advice with a fairly high degree of confidence about 'what works' in relation to effective partnership processes. However, definitive answers to the absolutely central question: what is the impact of partnership working? are much more difficult to find. Most evaluations of partnerships have focused on partnership processes rather than outcomes. Where outcomes have been considered the focus has been predominantly on the outcomes of *programmes*; there have been few attempts to answer the much more challenging follow-on question: to what extent did the *partnership* contribute to these outcomes? Perhaps the wide-spread assumption that partnerships are 'a good thing' has shifted the focus away from the difference that partnerships make to outcomes, towards how to make part-nership working itself more effective. Nevertheless, partnership working does bring with it significant costs in terms of the time and resources needed to make them work. Those costs do need to be justified in terms of the benefits to which they contribute. This requires a focus not just on outcomes but on the extent to which those outcomes can be attributed to partnership working.

Partnership working offers opportunities to go beyond planning and delivering existing services for children and young people in a more integrated and effective way, although this is an important first step. Rather, at their most creative, strategic partnerships should allow us to conceptualise what children and young people need and how those needs can best be met, in new and different ways. Central to this reconceptualisation should be a vision of the kinds of outcomes that we are seeking for children and young people and that they themselves want and need. The challenge, then, is for strategic partnerships to overcome the barriers to collaboration that they are likely to face and to release the creativity that can arise from diversity.

Resources

General guides and toolkits

Audit Commission (1998) *A fruitful partnership: effective partnership working.* **Audit Commission, London**

This guide to partnership working is based on fieldwork in 14 different partnerships. It addresses issues of relevance to the different stages of partnership development and provides useful case studies and checklists.

Department of Health (2002) Keys to partnership. www.doh.gov.uk/ learningdisabilities/

A guide to partnership working for local learning disability partnerships. It is organised around the following themes: the policy framework; what do we know about making partnerships work?; auditing the state of your partnership; partnership boards – making them work; practitioner partnerships; person-centred planning; structuring partnership arrangements in the field of learning disability; handy hints on working with key stakeholders.

Health Development Agency (2003) *The working partnership. Book 1: Introduction.* **Health Development Agency, London.**

Health Development Agency (2003) *The working partnership. Book 2: Short assessment.* **Health Development Agency, London.**

Health Development Agency (2003) *The working partnership. Book 3: In-depth assessment.* **Health Development Agency, London.**

These three publications provide, in varying depth and detail, a toolkit for assessing and improving partnership practice by taking users through the various stages of and issues associated with partnership development.

Markwell, S (2003) *Partnership working: a consumer guide to resources.* **Health Development Agency, London.**

Provides an overview of resources organised around three categories: toolkits; audits; and guides.

www.ourpartnership.org.uk

An e-project led by the National Council for Voluntary Organisations (NCVO) and Centre for Management and Policy Studies (CMPS). It has been developed for those in the voluntary, public and private sectors who are involved in delivering public services through partnerships. It aims to effect an exchange of skills and competencies between the public and voluntary sectors in order to build and sustain community-based services and partnership. The website provides easily accessible information; advice; case studies and opportunities to exchange and learn from experiences.

Thorlby, T, Hutchinson, J (2002) *Working in partnership: a sourcebook.* **New Opportunities Fund, London. Can be downloaded from www.nof.org.uk**

This toolkit draws on established good practice and research taken from 12 case studies of partnerships around the UK. The toolkit is designed to take the user through the main stages of partnership development and to help them think through the issues of relevance at each stage. It is aimed at organisations seeking funding from the New Opportunities Fund; however, it is of relevance to a wide range of partnerships.

Community and voluntary sector involvement

Clark, C (2004) *Community participation: a self-assessment toolkit for partnerships.* **Engage East Midlands, Nottingham.** Also available at http://www.engage-em.org.uk.

This is a self-assessment toolkit to support greater community and voluntary sector participation in regeneration partnerships. It adopts a partnership life-cycle approach and provides self-assessment tools for the following phases: start up; planning; implementation; evaluation; and renewal.

The **Community Development Foundation** (CDF, www.cdf.org.uk) produces a range of publications to support community and voluntary sector activity. The following are especially useful:

Chanan, G, Garratt, C, West, A (2000) *The new community strategies: how to involve local people.* CDF, London.

Community Development Foundation (2001) *The LSP guide: a handy guide to getting involved for voluntary and community groups.* CDF, London.

Henderson, P (2003) *Choice: examples of community participation methods in Europe.* CDF, London.

Wilcox, D (1994) *The guide to effective participation.* **Partnership, Brighton.**

A guide to community participation organised around key topics and an A–Z of issues and methods. It also provides a 'bridge' between theory and practice and guidance on developing participation strategies. See also the more recent **Wilcox, D (1998)** *Introduction to partnerships,* **http://www.partnerships.org.uk/AZP/part. html**

Wilson, A, Charlton, K (1997) *Making partnerships work: a practical guide for the public, private, voluntary and community sectors.* **Joseph Rowntree Foundation, York.**

This guide provides practical advice to managers on how to work effectively in partnership across sectors. Key lessons and experiences are cited drawing on the research that underpinned the production of the guide.

Involving children and young people

Children and Young People's Unit (2001) *Learning to listen. Core principles for the involvement of children and young people.* **DfES, London. Also available on the CYPU website: www.dfes.gov.uk/cypu**

Connexions (2002) *Good practice guide on involving young people in the governance of Connexions as decision-makers.* **DfES, Nottingham**

This guide is aimed at all those responsible for involving young people as decision-makers in the governance of Connexions but much of the content has wider applicability. The purpose of the guide is to:

- help partnerships to discuss and critically consider the best ways of ensuring that young people can be actively and meaningfully involved in the governance of Connexions
- help partnerships to work with young people and prepare them for active involvement in decision-making at whatever level is felt to be best for the partnership and young people
- provide support and resource material to partnerships to work with young people to involve them in the governance of the Connexions partnership.

Kirby, P, Bryson, S (2002) *Measuring the magic? Evaluating and researching young people's participation in public decision making.* **Carnegie Young People Initiative, London.**

This report examines how young people's participation in decision making can be evaluated. It provides advice and guidance on techniques and approaches to participation and includes checklists of 'do's and don'ts'.

Miller, J (1996) *Never too young: how young children can take responsibility and make decisions.* **Save the Children/National Early Years Network, London.**

Practical resource showing how children under eight can participate, make decisions and take responsibility for their actions. It provides early years workers with information about why participation works, and includes a range of tried and tested techniques for involving children.

Shepherd, C, Treseder, P (2002) *Participation – spice it up!* **Save the Children, London.**

This manual provides practical tools for engaging children and young people in planning and consultations. It is based on activities used with children and young people from 18 months to 25 years in a range of settings.

Wade, H, Badham, B (2003) Hear by right: standards for the active involvement of children and young people. National Youth Agency/Local Government Association, London.

A package of material including a book and CD-Rom offering standards for organisations to assess and improve practice and policy on the active involvement of children and young people.

Bibliography

6, Perri, Leat, D, Seltzer, K, Stoker, G (1999) *Governing in the round: strategies for holistic government.* Demos, London.

6, Perri, Leat, D, Seltzer, K, Stoker, G (2002) *Towards holistic governance. The new reform agenda.* Palgrave, Basingstoke.

Accounts Commission (2000) *How are we doing? Measuring the performance of community safety partnerships.* Audit Scotland, Edinburgh.

Arc Research and Consultancy Ltd (2002) *Right fit. Working it out: getting the most from partnerships.* Barkingside, Barnardo's.

Atkinson, M, Wilkin, A, Stott, A, Doherty, P, Kinder, K (2002) *Multi-agency working: a detailed study.* LGA Research Report 26. NFER, Slough.

Audit Commission (1998a) *A fruitful partnership.* Audit Commission, London.

Audit Commission (1998b) *Promising beginnings: a compendium of initiatives to improve joint working in local government.* Audit Commission, London.

Audit Commission (2003a) *Services for disabled children: a review of services for disabled children and their families.* Audit Commission, London.

Bailey, N (2003) Local strategic partnerships in England: the continuing search for collaborative advantage, leadership and strategy in urban governance. *Planning, Theory and Practice* 4(4): 443–457.

Bessant, J (2003) Youth participation: a new mode of government. *Policy Studies* 24(2/3): 87–100.

Bradshaw, J (ed) (2001) *Poverty: the outcomes for children.* Family Policy Studies Centre/National Children's Bureau, London.

Bradshaw, J (ed) (2002) *The well-being of children in the UK.* Save the Children, London.

Cabinet Office (2000) *Wiring it up: Whitehall's management of cross-cutting policies and services.* Performance and Innovation Unit, London.

Campbell, M, Percy-Smith, J (2000) *Partnership for success. A guide to partnership working for learning partnerships.* DfEE, London.

Carley, M, Chapman, M, Hastings, A, Kirk, K, Young, R (2000) *Urban regeneration through partnership: a study in nine urban regions in England, Scotland and Wales.* Policy Press, Bristol.

Children and Young People's Unit (2001a) *Building a strategy for children and young People.* CYPU, London.

Children and Young People's Unit (2001b) *Learning to listen: core principles for the involvement of children and young people.* CYPU, London.

Children and Young People's Unit (2003) *Changing futures.* Annual report of the Children and Young People's Unit. DfES, London.

Civic Trust (1999) *Winning partnerships for voluntary and community groups: a guide to working with cross-sectoral regeneration partnerships.* Civic Trust, London.

Connell, JP, Kubisch, AC (1998) Applying a theory of change approach to the evaluation of comprehensive community initiatives: progress, prospects and problems. In Fulbright-Anderson, K, Kubisch, AC, Connell, JP (eds) *New approaches to evaluating community initiatives. Vol. 2: Theory, measurement and analysis.* Aspen Institute, Washington DC.

Connexions (2002) *Good practice guide on involving young people in the governance of Connexions as decision-makers.* DfES, Nottingham.

Cutler, D, Frost, R (2001) *Taking the initiative: promoting young people's involvement in public decision-making in the UK.* Carnegie Young People Initiative, London.

Dean, J, Hastings, A, More, A, Young, R (1999) *Fitting together? A study of partnership processes in Scotland.* Scottish Homes, Edinburgh.

Department for Education and Skills (2004) *Every child matters: next steps.* DfES, London.

Department for Education and Skills, Department of Health, Home Office (2003) *Keeping children safe: the government's response to the Victoria Climbié Inquiry Report and Joint Chief Inspectors' report Safeguarding Children*, Cm 5861. The Stationery Office, London.

Department of the Environment, Transport and the Regions (1999a) *Cross-cutting issues affecting local government.* DETR, London.

Department of the Environment , Transport and the Regions (1999b) *'Cross-cutting issues in public policy and public services.* DETR, London.

Department of the Environment, Transport and the Regions (2000a) *Report of Policy Action Team 17, joining it up locally.* The Stationery Office, London.

Department of the Environment, Transport and the Regions (2000b) *Newchurch Series,* www.local-regions.detr.gov.uk/research/newchurch/

Department of Health (2001) *Valuing people: a new strategy for learning disability for the 21st century.* Cm 5086. The Stationery Office, London.

Department of Health (2002a) *Keys to partnership. Working together to make a difference in people's lives.* Department of Health, London.

Department of Health (2002b) *Promoting the health of looked after children.* Department of Health, London.

Department of Health (2002c) *Consultation on new guidance on children's services planning.* Department of Health, London.

Department of Health (2003a) *The standard for hospital services* and *NSF emerging findings,* www.doh.gov.uk/nsf/children/gettingtherightstart.htm

Department of Health (2003b) *Involving children and young people – an introduction.* Department of Health, London.

Department of Health/Department for Education and Skills (2004) *National Service Framework for Children, Young People and Maternity Services.* Department of Health, London.

Department of Health, Home Office, Department for Education and Employment, National Assembly for Wales (1999) *Working together to safeguard children.* The Stationery Office, London.

Department of Health, Department for Education and Employment, Home Office (2000) *Framework for the assessment of children in need and their families.* The Stationery Office, London.

Department of Health/Home Office (2003) *The Victoria Climbié report of an inquiry by Lord Laming*, www.victoria-climbie-inquiry.org.uk/finreport/finreport.htm

Frearson, A (2002) *Partnership self-assessment toolkit*, available to download at www.haznet.org.uk/hazs/hazmap/leeds_partner-tool.pdf

Frye, M, Webb, A (2002) *Effective partnership working*. The Public Inquiry Unit, London.

Gardner, R (2003) Working together to improve children's life-chances: the challenge of inter-agency collaboration. In Weinstein, J, Whittington, C, Leiba, T (eds) *Collaboration in social work practice*. Jessica Kingsley, London.

Gaster, L, Deakin, N, Riseborough, M, McAbe, A, Wainwright, S, Rogers, H (1999) *History, strategy or lottery? The realities of local government/voluntary sector relationships*. Improvement and Development Agency, London.

Glendinning, C, Powell, M, Rummery, K (eds) (2002) *Partnerships, new Labour and the governance of welfare*. Policy Press, Bristol.

Goss, S (2001) *Making local governance work. Networks, relationships and the management of change*. Palgrave, Basingstoke.

Guba, EG, Lincoln, YS (1981) *Effective evaluation*. Jossey-Bass, London.

Hamer, L, Smithies, J (2002) *Planning across the local strategic partnership (LSP). Case studies of integrating community strategies and health improvement*. Health Development Agency, London.

Harding, A, Fordham, G, Evans, R, Fordham, R, Harrison, A, Parkinson, M (1998) *Building partnerships in the English regions. A study report of regional and sub-regional partnerships in England*. DETR, London.

Hardy, B, Hudson, B, Waddington, E (2000) *What makes a good partnership? A partnership assessment tool*. Nuffield Institute for Health, London.

Harrison, R, Mann, G, Murphy, M, Taylor, A, Thompson, N (2003) *Partnership made painless: a joined up guide to working together*. Russell House Publishing, Lyme Regis.

Health Development Agency (2003a) *The working partnership. Book 1: Introduction.* Health Development Agency, London.

Health Development Agency (2003b) *The working partnership. Book 2: Short assessment.* Health Development Agency, London.

Health Development Agency (2003c) *The working partnership. Book 3: In-depth assessment.* Health Development Agency, London.

Hogg, K (2000) *Making a difference: effective implementation of cross-cutting policy.* Scottish Executive Policy Unit, Edinburgh.

Howarth, C, Kenway, P, Palmer, G, Miorelli, R (1999) *Monitoring poverty and social exclusion 1999.* New Policy Institute/Joseph Rowntree Foundation, York.

Hudson, B, Hardy, B (2002) What is a 'successful' partnership and how can it be measured? In Glendinning, C, Powell, M, Rummery, K (eds) *Partnerships, new Labour and the governance of welfare.* Policy Press, Bristol.

Hughes, L (2003) Developing primary care services for young people. *British Journal of Family Planning* 26(3): 155–160.

Huxham, C (ed) (1996) *Creating collaborative advantage.* Sage, London.

Hutchinson, J, Campbell, M (1998) *Working in partnership: lessons from the literature.* DfEE Research report RR63. DfEE, London.

Integrated Care Network (2003) *Integrated working and governance: a discussion paper.* Integrated Care Network, Leeds.

Joint Chief Inspectors (2002) *Safeguarding children.* Department of Health, London.

Kelly, G (2000) *The new partnership agenda.* IPPR, London.

Kirby, P, Bryson, S (2002) *Measuring the magic? Evaluating and researching young people's participation in public decision making.* Carnegie Young People Initiative, London.

Leiba, T, Weinstein, J (2003) Who are the participants in the collaborative process and what makes collaboration succeed or fail? In Weinstein, J, Whittington, C, Leiba, T (eds) *Collaboration in social work practice.* Jessica Kingsley, London.

Lewis, J, Utting, D (2001) Made to measure? Evaluating community initiatives for children. *Children and Society* 15(1): 1–4.

Local Government Association (1999) *Take your partners: report of the LGA urban commission hearings into partnership working*. Local Government Association, London.

Lowndes, V, Nanton, P, McCabe, A, Skelcher, C (1997) Networks, partnerships and urban regeneration. *Local Economy* 11(4): 333–343.

Lowndes, V, Skelcher, C (1998) The dynamics of multi-organisational partnerships: an analysis of changing modes of governance. *Public Administration* 76, Summer: 313–333.

McArthur, A (1995) The active involvement of local residents in strategic community partnerships. *Policy and Politics* 23(1): 61–71.

McNeish, D, Newman, T (2002) What works in involving children in decision-making. In McNeish, D, Newman, T, Roberts, H (eds) *What works for children: effective services for children and families*. Open University Press, Buckingham.

Markwell, S (2003) *Partnership working. A consumer guide to resources*. Health Development Agency, London.

Miller, C (2003) *The organisational implications of the children's services Green Paper*. Office for Public Management, London.

Morris, K, Spicer, N (2003) *The national evaluation of the Children's Fund: early messages from developing practice*. University of Birmingham, Birmingham (also at: www.ne-cf.org).

National Audit Office (2001) *Joining up to improve public services*. National Audit Office, London.

NCVO, Local Government Management Board (1993) *Building effective local partnerships*. NCVO/LGMB, London.

NHS executive (2000) *Working in partnership: developing a whole systems approach. Good practice guide*. NHS Executive, London.

Office of the Deputy Prime Minister, Department for Transport (2003) *Evaluation of local strategic partnerships*. Office of the Deputy Prime Minister/Department for Transport, London.

Ofsted, Audit Commission, Social Services Inspectorate (2003) *The Children's Fund first wave partnerships*. Ofsted/Audit Commission/SSI, London.

Osborne, SP (1997) Voluntary organizations and partnerships in local community economic development. The role of Local Development Agencies. *Local Economy* 12(4): 290–295.

Pawson, R, Tilley, N (1997) *Realistic evaluation*. Sage, London.

Pettit, B (2003) *Effective joint working between child and adolescent mental health services (CAMHS) and schools*. Research Report RR412. DfES, London.

Pharoah, C, Romney-Alexander, D, Kemp, K, Smerdon, M (1998) *Achieving the double bottom line: a study of the voluntary and community sector in regeneration partnerships*. CAF, Kent.

Pollitt, C (2003) Joined-up government: a survey. *Political Studies Review* 1(1), January: 34–49.

Powell, M, Glendinning, C (2002) Introduction. In Glendinning, C, Powell, M, Rummery, K (eds) *Partnerships, new Labour and the governance of welfare*. Policy Press, Bristol.

Prime Minister, Minister for the Cabinet Office (1999) *Modernising government, Cm4310*. The Stationery Office, London.

Rahman, M, Palmer, G, Kenway, P, Howard, C (2000) *Monitoring poverty and social exclusion, 2000*. Joseph Rowntree Foundation, York.

Rahman, M, Palmer, G, Kenway, P (2001) *Monitoring poverty and social exclusion, 2001*. Joseph Rowntree Foundation, York.

Ranade, W, Hudson, B (2004) Conceptual issues in inter-agency collaboration. *Local Government Studies* 29(3): 32–50.

renewal.net (2002) *Build a partnership*, www.renewal.net

Richards, S, Barnes, M, Coulson, C, Gaster, L, Leach, B, Sullivan, H (1999) *Cross-cutting issues in public policy and public service.* DETR, London.

Roaf, C (2002) *Joined up action. Co-ordinating services for included children.* Open University Press, Buckingham.

Roberts, V, Russell, H, Harding, A, Parkinson, M (1995) *Public private voluntary partnerships in local government.* Local Government Management Board, Luton.

Roxburgh, I, Arend, N (2003) *Crossing boundaries: new ways of working.* New Local Government Network, London.

Russell, H, Dawson, J, Garside, P, Parkinson, M (1996) *City Challenge interim evaluation.* The Stationery Office, London.

Scottish Executive (2002) *Beyond boundaries. A development approach to improving inter-agency working.* Scottish Executive, Edinburgh.

Scottish Office (1996) *Partnership in the regeneration of urban Scotland.* Scottish Office, Central Research Unit, Edinburgh.

Social Services Inspectorate (2002) *Delivering quality children's services – inspection of children's services.* Department of Health, London.

Stoney, S, West, A, Kendall, L, Morris, M (2002) *Evaluation of excellence in cities: overview of interim findings.* NFER, London.

Sullivan, H, Skelcher, C (2002) *Working across boundaries. Collaboration in public services.* Palgrave, Basingstoke.

Sutherland, H, Sefton, T, Piachaud, D (2003) *Poverty in Britain: the impact of government policy since 1997.* Joseph Rowntree Foundation, York.

Taylor, M (2000) Communities in the lead: power, organisational capacity and social capital. *Urban Studies* 37(5–6): 1019–1035.

Thorlby, T, Hutchinson, J (2002) *Working in partnership: a sourcebook.* New Opportunities Fund, London.

Tomlinson, K (2003) *Effective inter-agency working: a review of the literature and examples from practice.* LGA Research Report 40. National Foundation for Educational Research, Slough.

HM Treasury (2001) *Cross-cutting review of children at risk.* The Stationery Office, London.

HM Treasury (2003) *Every child matters, Cm 5860.* The Stationery Office, London.

Webb, R, Vulliamy, G (2001) Joining up the solutions: the rhetoric and practice of inter-agency co-operation. *Children and Society* 15: 315–332.

Weinstein, J, Whittington, C, Leiba, T (eds) (2003) *Collaboration in social work practice.* Jessica Kingsley, London.

Whittington, C (2003a) Collaboration and partnership in context. In Weinstein, J, Whittington, C, Leiba, T (eds) *Collaboration in social work practice.* Jessica Kingsley, London.

Whittington, C (2003) A model of collaboration. In Weinstein, J, Whittington, C, Leiba, T (eds) *Collaboration in social work practice.* Jessica Kingsley, London.

Wilcox, D (1994) *The guide to effective participation.* Partnership, Brighton.

Wilcox, D (1998) *Introduction to partnerships* www.partnerships.org.uk/AZP/part.html

Wilkinson, M, Craig, G (2002) *New roles for old: local authority members and partnership working.* Joseph Rowntree Foundation, York.

Willow, C (2002) *Participation in practice. Children and young people as partners in change.* The Children's Society, London.

Wilson, A, Charlton, K (1997) *Making partnership work: a practical guide for the public, private, voluntary and community sectors.* Joseph Rowntree Foundation, York.

Wilson, V, Pirie, A (2000) *Multi-disciplinary team working: beyond the barriers? A review of the issues.* SCRE, Edinburgh.

Index